TABLE OF CONTENTS.

INSTRUCTIONS FOR TAKING DESCRIPTIONS.

PART FIRST.

ANTHROPOMETRIC INFORMATION.

CHAPTER I.

Measurements performed by means of the Caliper-Compasses (Cranium diameters).

CHAPTER II.

Measurements taken by means of the Sliding Compasses.

CHAPTER III.

Measurements taken by means of the Vertical and Horizontal Graduated Measures.

PART SECOND.

―――

PART THIRD.

THE UNIVERSITY OF
WINCHESTER

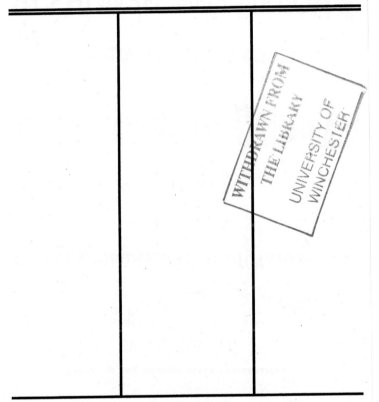
With an Historical and Explanatory Introduction
by the Translator.

1889.

INTRODUCTION.

In 1881 when the question of deportation of habitual criminals agitated the minds of the French people, and was discussed in parliament, Mons. Alphonse Bertillon first presented to the public of Paris an idea of a method of describing persons and identifying individuals, vastly superior to the old one with its vague indications of a person's height, the color of his hair and eyes, his complexion, the size or form of his nose, chin, forehead, etc.

DEFECTS OF THE OLD METHOD.

In the "Annales de Demographie Internationale," Mons. Bertillon stated, from personal measurements and observations made in Paris with over 10,000 subjects, that among a hundred persons of same height thus observed,

    87 had what is commonly called " brown " hair.

    10 " blonde hair.

    2.7 " black   "

    0.3 (3 in every 1000) had red hair.

A person with "brown" hair has, therefore, no distinction from nine-tenths of the total population. In other words, in 9 out of 10 times a description of the color of the hair would be useless, or nearly so. The color of the hair, therefore, has a characteristic descriptive power only with the blonde, black and red headed. One might as well,—in a lesser proportion, require a man's description to state whether he was a hunchback or not. An individual ranged in the category of non-hunchbacks would have this characteristic common with 9999 out of every 10,000 persons.

This irregularity of repartition is still more striking when considered in connection with the epithets "long, large, medium, small," etc., which, in ordinary descriptions, mean to convey an idea of the appearance of the nose, forehead, mouth, etc. One sees hardly anything else but "medium;" and what appears small to one to-day, may to-morrow be described as large by another.

Similar difficulties appear in the description of the color of the eye; one third of the subjects observed of even height having hazel eyes; one-fourth what is commonly styled gray; one-seventh blue, and one-fourth of indistinct color.

The same with the height. Nearly one-third of all measured range, within the small limit, between 1 m. 65 to 1 m. 70, one-third from the dwarf to 1 m. 65, and one-third from 1 m. 70, to the giant.

These are the principal features of the old style descriptions.

Photographs are undoubtedly a great aid in establishing the identity of an individual. But it is very difficult, almost impossible, to find in a large collection the picture of a person without knowing his name. A photograph is valuable in *verifying* the identity of an individual, but it is altogether impotent to help you *discover* this identity, if you have no other means but your eyes to search for the photograph among the thousands in an ordinary collection.

THE BERTILLON METHOD.

All these difficulties are obviated by the new Bertillon method of identification, the measurement and subsequent classification and subdivision of such parts of the human body as do not change in size after a person has attained his full growth (at the age of 20 to 22 years), such as the length and width of the head, the length of the middle and little fingers, the length of the foot, forearm, etc., the height of the figure, the measurement of the outstretched arms, and the trunk of a person seated, etc. A man individualized by measurements of this character is *mathematically* identified.

It is altogether unlikely that among many thousand subjects, *two* will be found who will *approximately* reveal figures of the same head diameters, the same foot, finger, etc. To find two subjects showing *exactly* the same anthropometric indications in every particular is just as great an impossibility as to discover two persons or objects that look exactly alike. When the eye cannot discover a distinction, figures " which will not lie," will certainly do it.

Suppose we have a collection of 60,000 photographs of men, and divide them into three equal groups, according to the measurement of the *length* of the head.

Those with small length, 20,000.
" " medium " 20,000.
" " large " 20,000.

To make these groups approximately equal it is evidently necessary that the series of medium length of head should be of less extent than those of large or small length, and should contain, for instance, only the individals measuring from 19 centimeters to 19.4 centimeters, (metrical system) *while that of large length should contain all the individuals measuring 19.5 and more, and that of small length all those measuring *less* than 19 centimeters.

The same rule is applicable to the classification of all measurements, as nature itself commends and treads the "golden midway" in preference to the abnormally small or large.

---

*Note.—The convenient French metrical system,—meter, decimeter, centimeter and millimeter,—is exclusively used in the application of the Bertillon method. For those wishing to transpose the French measure into that commonly used in the United States, the following formula will be of service :

1 U. S. inch=.025401 meter.
1 " foot = .30481 "
1 " yard=.914430 "

1 meter = 3.2809 U. S. ft.

13 inches=33 centimeters (practically.)
65 " =165.1 "

For the measurement of the " *height*" at the Joliet Penitentiary, a graduated measure is used, showing both the French and United States measures. (Meters, centimeters, etc., and corresponding feet and inches.)

Each one of these original divisions is then subdivided, on the same principle, without regard to the length of the head of the individual, into three groups according to the *width* of the head. These new subdivisions, numbering 3 × 3=9, would then contain those

> With heads of small width, 6000 photographs and over.
>   "   "   " medium "   6000   "   "   "
>   "   "   " large   "   6000   "   "   "

Experience proves that the width of the head of most people varies independently of the length. In other words, if the head of an individual measures a certain length, it does not necessarily follow that its width can—even approximately—be determined thereby.

The length of the *middle finger* will give a third indication, dividing the nine groups we already have into three groups each, making 27 groups in all, with the following result:

> Those with small middle finger, 2000 photographs.
>   "   " medium "   "   2000   "
>   "   " large   "   "   2000   "

Another subdivision by the measurement of the *foot* (in three classes—small, medium, and large) will reduce the 27 groups of 2,000 into 81 of over 600 each. Each will again be subdivided into still smaller groups, by taking the *forearm* as basis of subdivision. Another subdivision is effected by the measurement of the *height*, another by the *little finger*, the *ear*, etc. A division by the length of the forearm would give a quotient of 200, reduced by a division of the height to 66, again reduced by the little finger to 22, by the ear to 7, and so on. The meaning of all this is that by the means of eight co-efficient anthropometric measurements, each divided into three mathematically defined classes of small, medium, and large, a collection of as many as sixty thousand photographs could be divided into groups of no more than 7 or 8 photographs each, which it would be an easy matter to examine rapidly and carefully, and with desirable results.

Suppose, again, that a criminal is arrested under an assumed name, and we wish to ascertain whether he has been measured and photographed before. We take an exact measurement of the length of his head and will know at once in which of the main divisions we can find his name. The width of his head will lead us more specifically to the place his photograph can be found. The length of his middle finger, of his foot, forearm, height, little finger, ear, etc., will enable us to arrive at the exact place where his photograph and description have been filed,—if at all.

If a measurement coincides exactly with the figures on the limit of a division, the search has also to be made in the next higher or lower adjoining division.

Experience has demonstrated that the different parts of the human body are not by any means in constant congruity, one with each other. One person is of small stature, but has a large head and large feet; another has small feet and short fingers, but is of tall stature. The variations in individuals are so great, and the precision of the measurements so minute and perfect, that among a hundred thousand subjects there are hardly ten who will show approximate figures on every indication. But even these few can, by the description, according to the Bertillon method, of the eye and the nose, and the form and location of accidental scars and marks, be individualized, almost beyond a possible doubt or confusion.

If I know how to spell a word "Bread" for instance, and wish to find it and its definition in the dictionary,—I look first for the letter B, eliminating the 25 other letters of the alphabet; then I find R as a subdivision to B, then E as a subdivison to BR, then A and D in a similar way, until I find that very word in the *only* place in the dictionary where—if correctly spelled—it can properly be filed. Similar analyses and eliminations are made in searching for a description in an anthropometrical file, with results almost equally favorable.

The following pages of M. Bertillon's instructions for taking anthropometric descriptions will bear convincing testimony to the thorough and thoughtful manner in which he has treated his subject. Of necessity he enters minutely into the details of execution, but assures us that the practice of it is very simple, expeditious, and easily learned ; that it is an operation, the performance of which is within the range of the intelligence of an ordinary person, and requires but a few minutes' time.

If these indications are taken strictly according to instruc. tions, it is almost impossible for the operator to err or be mis- led by the subject. The experience had in this country bears out this assertion. No one should be dismayed at the extent and volume of the " Instructions," but the book ought not to be studied except with the instruments and a subject at hand.

HISTORICAL.

The history of the practical application of the Bertillon method of identification runs back—even in France—but a few years. Inaugurated by the Prefecture of Police in Paris at the end of 1882, 49 individuals were, *by this method exclusively*, recognized as habitual criminals in 1883, after all other means of identification had failed ; 241 were by the same means identified in 1884, and more than 500 in 1885.

The intrinsic value of the system, recognized and proven by such results, so strongly recommended itself to Mons. Herbette. Councillor of State and Director General of the Penitentiary administration in France (a branch of the Department of the Interior) that he lent M. Bertillon his powerful assistance in getting the system officially recognized and extended throughout France, where, in police as well as penitentiary circles it is now universally adopted and successfully practiced.*

In March, 1887, at Detroit, Mich., an association of Wardens and Superintendents of American prisons was formed with the avowed object " to secure the registration in a central

*I admire the results obtained, but what I admire still more is the fact, as unique, at least, and novel as the method itself, that an administration, leaving behind all its precedents and abandoning its past methods, should unhesitatingly step flat-footedly into a new one.—*Dr. Bordier, in the " Nationale," of Paris, on B.'s method of identification.*

office, of the criminal record of prisoners, so far as the same
may be known to prison officers, members of the association,
and the mutual interchange between prisons of such information, with a view to distinguishing between habitual and occa-
sional offenders, and as an aid to reformatory work in prisons."
At about the same date the writer, whose attention had been
called to the new French method by a short notice circulating
in the newspapers of the United States, put himself in commu-
nication with M. Bertillon at Paris, and was soon thereafter
in receipt of that gentleman's answer to his inquiries, together
with a few pamphlets describing the system and the details of
its working, also a letter from Mons. Herbette who not only
recommended in highest terms M. Bertillon's system, but testi-
fied to its successful practical operation in France, and urged
its adoption in the United States, with promises of the most
gratifying results.

Major R. W. McClaughrey, then Warden of the Illinois
State Penitentiary, and Secretary of the newly formed Wardens' Association, to whom for his moral and material support,
more than to any one else, the innovation owes its introduction
and fair progress in the United States, was at once convinced
of the immeasurable superiority of the Bertillon system of
identification to anything theretofore suggested or attempted in
that direction, and by circular letter invited and urged its
adoption in the United States by the wardens of prisons and
chiefs of police.

The French pamphlets treating on the subject, or parts of
them at least, were translated into English and brought before
the general public. Major McClaughrey then authorized the
purchase of a complete set of measuring instruments from
Paris, and practical operations were soon commenced at the
Illinois State Penitentiary at Joliet, under the supervision of
Mr. Moses H. Luke, who also, from the very start, proved to
be a willing and enthusiastic advocate of the system.

In the meanwhile Major McClaughrey succeeded in arousing
the interest of other prominent prison men in the new method.
Capt. Joseph Nicholson, Superintendent of the House of Cor-

rection at Detroit, Mich., and Charles E. Felton, Superintendent of the House of Correction at Chicago, Ill., warmly advocated and indorsed it, and the Bertillon System was finally adopted by the Wardens' Association of the United States and Canada, at their meeting at Toronto, in September, 1887.

A school of instruction was held at Joliet in February,1888, and attended by representatives from about ten or twelve prominent prisons, where the new system has since been put in practical operation. The Ohio Penitentiary at Columbus, the House of Correction at Detroit, the Western Penitentiary of Pennsylvania, the New Jersey State Prison at Trenton, the Central Prison at Toronto, Canada, and others, report fair and gratifying success in the undertaking.

The public press in various parts of the country has from time to time favorably commented on the system as practised in the United States. Professors of colleges and universities have looked into its working, and pronounced it a success. Officers of the army are seriously considering it with a view of advocating its adoption for the identification of deserters; and departments of police all over this broad land are beginning to appreciate its merits, and to predict its general adoption. The Bertillon System is in a fair way of becoming a fixture of permanent and universal usefulness in the United States and Canada.

Very little as yet can be said regarding its *practical* results in this country. During the one year and four months the Bertillon measurements have been taken and filed at the Joliet Penitentiary but few discharged convicts have re-entered the prison. They have however, been recognized as recidivists by remeasurement identical, or nearly so, with their anterior description. Of over 1,400 photographs now classified and filed in the Joliet collection, or placed on its index,* *any one* can be

---

* To avoid the more bulky and cumbersome boxes for filing photographs and descriptive cards, Mr. M. H. Luke of the Joliet Penitentiary has published an Index as a companion to the Bertillon files,—"Division Index of Anthropometric Measurements and Descriptions. (Bertillon System.)" This index, arranged in a compact and convenient form, is based on the same classification and subdivisions, as the card and photograph files in boxes, and leads in a similar way to the desired result of finding a subject from a given description.

ɔometrical
ent among
es for the
en claimed

ɔ utility of
als, and in
ι the occa-
acilities in
ιe wardens
endents of

curate and
od affords,
ffender, by
ɔ files with
acious and
on method
ɔ than any
rson. The
on method
again to be
resurrected or examined unless called forth by a duplicate
description taken from the identical person and occasioned by
a subsequent offence.

The general utility of the system cannot be better eluci-
dated than by quoting some of the remarks made concerning
it by *Mons. Herbette* at the International Prison Congress at
Rome, in November, 1885.

He set forth all the services already rendered by the system
of Anthropometric Descriptions, together with those that it
would yet be called on to perform.

He dwelt upon the assistance that the system could be
called upon to render toward identifying international male-
factors, who so readily adopt names and countries other than
their own. Crime becoming in some sort professional, and as

it were a specialty in the hands of a few individuals who know how to profit by the progress of civilization, and escape repression, it is natural that society should, in retaliation, avail itself of the discoveries of science in order to baffle their schemes.

The application of M. Bertillon's method has justified the hopes it inspired. At Paris, at Versailles, at Melun, at Poissy, at Lyons, etc., the system is adopted in its integrity. A few days have sufficed to teach it to the guards and officers in charge.

Ascending to more general considerations, and praising the successful efforts of M. Bertillon, M. Herbette demonstrated how this ascertainment of the physical personality and undeniable identity of individuals, arrived at an adult age, may be made to answer for needs the most real, and services the most varied. Should it be a question, for example, of giving to the inhabitants of a country, the soldiers of an army, or travelers visiting the most distant lands, individual descriptions or charts of peculiar marks, enabling them to identify themselves, or be recognized at all times; should it be a question of preventing false impersonations; should it be a question of recording all the distinctive marks of an individual on bank drafts and letters of credit, or in documents, titles and contracts, where it is desirable that his personality should be established, for his own interest, for the interest of third parties, or for the interest of the State—the system of anthropometric descriptions will in each instance find its proper office. Should there be a certificate of life, a policy of life insurance, or occasionally a certificate of death to be drawn up; should there be something needed to certify to the identity of an insane or unconscious person who may be seriously wounded or disfigured so that he can hardly be recognized; in case of sudden or violent death, the result of crime, of accident, of shipwreck, of battle, how serviceable it would be to trace these private marks, unchangeable in each individual, endlessly variable between individuals, indelible, in part at least, until death.

The advantage of it would be still more manifest if it were necessary to establish the identity of people far away, after a lapse of time, when their external appearance, their physiognomy, their features and physical habits have become changed, either naturally or artificially; and that without removal or expense, by a simple exchange of notes or figures forwarded from one country to another, from one continent to another, in a manner to make it known in the United States who such a man is who came from France, and to ascertain whether such and such a traveler met with at Rome is indeed the same person who was measured at Stockholm ten years before.

In a word, to fix the human personality, to give each human being an identity, an individuality, certain, durable, invariable, always recognizable, and always capable of being proven; such seems to be the broadest aim of the new method.

It may be said in consequence, that the range of the problem, as well as the importance of its solution, passes far beyond the limits of penitentiary work, and of the interest (although quite considerable) in the action to be taken on penal questions by the various nations.

Such are the motives that have induced us to give the labors of M. Bertillon, and their practical usefulness, the publicity that befits them.

In conclusion, one thing more ought not to be lost sight of. I quote M. Bertillon's own words:

"Although the details of the system have been decided on, I would not refuse to adopt any new modification offering superior advantages, no matter how the change might affect the French collections to date. But I beg of the prison and police authorities of other countries, who are disposed to adopt the anthropometric system, *not to introduce special modifications of their own*, which would tend to destroy the uniformity of the system, when it is an easy matter for all to act in concert as regards the different measurements to be taken, the choice of instruments, and the modus operandi.

"It is at the very outset of these questions that we must lay the foundation for the future internationalization of the system, without waiting for routine on one hand, and the yearly accu-

mulations of dissimilar informations on the other, to put insur-
mountable obstacles in the way."*

GALLUS MULLER,
Clerk Ill. State Penitentiary,
JOLIET, ILL., January, 1889.

---

* NOTE.—The non-universality of the metric system is no obstacle whatever to
this internationalization. In countries where this system is not in use, the figures on
our instruments are simply taken, not as actual measures of length, etc., but as ciphers
or signs designating a certain information sought for. Not the length, as such, is of
importance to us, but the figures indicating wherein it differs from other measures.
The main object is to make the interchange as rapidly, and with as few complications
as possible.

GENERAL OBSERVATIONS

ON

ANTHROPOMETRIC IDENTIFICATION.

(By Alphonse Bertillon.)

———————

1. The identification of a prisoner rests upon the knowledge of the following indications:

    1. The length and width of the head.
    2. The length of the left, middle. and little fingers.
    3. The length of the left foot.
    4. The length of the left fore-arm.
    5. The length of the right ear.
    6. The height of the figure.
    7. The measurement of the outstretched arms.
    8. The measurement of the trunk, i. e., measurement from the bench to the top of the head of a person seated.

2. It is proper to add to these principal indications the description of the scars and peculiar marks that every individual more or less exhibits, and for a collection of cards of description without photographs, the notation, according to a special vocabulary, of the color of the eye, hair and beard, as well as the form and dimensions of the nose.*

———————

NOTE.—Following is the order in which these measurements and descriptions are taken at the Joliet Penitentiary, the prisoner being brought into the operating room barefooted, and in shirt sleeves.

1. THE HEIGHT.—The measurement of the person standing erect.
2. THE OUTSTRETCHED ARMS.—The measurement from finger tip to finger tip, the arms being extended in a right-angular cross with the body.

17

18

3. These different operations necessitate the use of special instruments called caliper-compasses (Fig. 1) and sliding compasses (Figs. 2, 3), and of three graduated measures permanently fastened to a suitable wall, two being placed vertically and one horizontally (Fig. 4).

4. The caliper compasses are intended exclusively for measuring the cranium diameters, for which operation they are found to be more convenient and precise than the sliding compasses.

5. The very minute directions given in another part should be carefully observed in all their details, but it would be a mistake to think it necessary to commit the text to memory.

6. The simplest way to learn how to measure without the teacher's help is to practise at first on a fellow officer or other willing subject, using the photographs annexed to the instructions as guides for each movement. The part the printed text is intended to perform, is to attract the attention of the apprentice to the nice points, and to verify the movements and positions.

7. From the very first exercise of this kind it will be apparent that any one movement requiring ten lines of description can be executed in the easiest and most natural manner in a half second.

8. The figures obtained on the same individual at different sittings should be compared and these preparatory exercises

----

3. THE TRUNK.—The measurement from the bench to the top of the head of a person seated.

These three measurements are taken by means of the perpendicular and horizontal graduated measures placed on the wall.

4. THE LENGTH OF THE HEAD.—Measurement from the cavity at the root of the nose to the remotest point of the back of the head.

5 THE WIDTH OF THE HEAD.—Measurement of the diameter from side to side between the two points most remote from each other, situated over the ears and on a horizontal plane at right angles to the measurement of length.

Measurements 3 and 4 are taken by means of the caliper compasses.

6. THE RIGHT EAR.—Measurement from the top of the rim to the lowest point of the lobe.

This measurement is taken by means of the small sliding compasses.

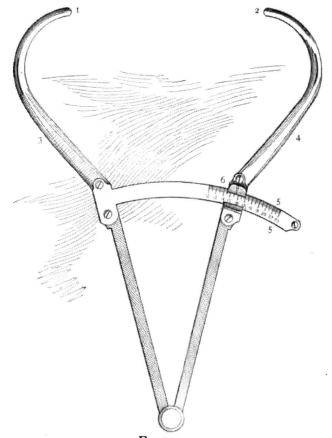

FIGURE 1.
CALIPER COMPASSES,

For measuring the length and the width of the head.

Read the indication directly under the Zero-Dart on the sliding branch.

1. Left extremity.
2. Right extremity
3. Left arm or branch.
4. Right arm or branch.

5. Graduated bar.
6. Index on zero-dart.
   Set-screw on reverse side.

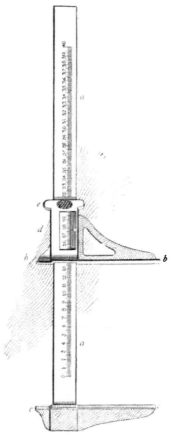

FIGURE 2.

SLIDING COMPASSES,

For measuring the foot, forearm, and middle and little fingers.

Read the indication directly opposite the Zero-Dart on the sliding branch

a. Shank.
b b. Small and large sliding branches.
c c. Small and large stationary branches.

d. Zero-Dart or index.
e. Button for moving the slide.

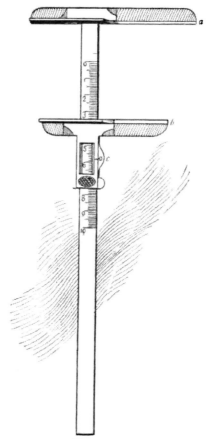

FIGURE 3.

SMALL SLIDING COMPASSES,

For Measuring the Ear.

Read the indication directly opposite the zero-dart on the sliding branch.

a. Stationary branch.
b. Sliding branch.
c. Zero dart, or index.

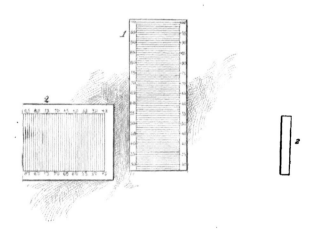

FIGURE 4.

1. **VERTICAL MEASURE,**
For the height.

2—2. **HORIZONTAL MEASURE,**
For the outstretched arms.

3. **SQUARE,**
For measurement of height and trunk.

continued until the *differences observed do not exceed in any instance the approximate figures indicated for each measurement.*

9. As two or three of the measurements can be modified or influenced by trickery on the part of the subject, it would be well for the operator himself to practice the motions that are apt to alter the result, and to allow his assistants to do the same, so that he may be able to easily discover these trickeries whenever they occur in actual practice.

10. Of course these exercises should not be practised when prisoners are present. We will indicate, however, at the end of each chapter of the rules, the tricks and mistakes against which one has to guard himself in each measurement.

11. As a rule the operator must never let the prisoner suppose that deception can be successfully practised. He must correct the trickeries, or execute movements that will prevent them, without any explanation whatever.

12. Two or three lessons ordinarily suffice to make an operator tolerably proficient.

13. Not taking into account the time needed to ascertain either the civil status of a prisoner (name, occupation, domicile, date of birth, etc.), or the many various particular marks of the subject (scars, moles, etc.), the simple process of measuring, after the period of groping has been passed, will not require more than four or five minutes per subject.

14. As much light as possible should be admitted into the operating room, which ought to be floored with wood, or carpeted.

15. In the beginning the assistant, as well as the operator,

---

7. THE LEFT FOOT.—Measurement from the extreme point of the back of the heel to the end of the farthest projecting toe.

8. THE LEFT MIDDLE FINGER.—Measurement from the point of the knuckle to the tip of the finger, the finger being placed at right angles to the back of the hand.

9. THE LEFT LITTLE FINGER.—Same as for middle finger.

10. THE LEFT FOREARM.—Measurement from the point of the elbow to the tip of the farthest projecting finger, the elbow being placed at sharp angles with the upper arm.

Measurements 7, 8, 9 and 10 are taken by means of the large sliding compasses.

should take the measurements, in order to make sure that the differences between one operation and the other of a certain measurement do not exceed the prescribed limits of approximation. This check becomes less necessary when the experience of several weeks has demonstrated that divergencies in measure or error in dictation no longer occur.

16. To become efficient in this work the operator should know unmistakably the nearest approximation to which each measurement, or more generally speaking each indication, can be ascertained.

17. In this matter one must reason in the same way as is done daily with regard to a person's stature. You will never confound an individual measuring 1 meter 60 in height with one measuring 1-70.

18. Thus if the officer taking or comparing descriptions knows to a certainty that the length of the head, for instance, never exceeds an approximation of two millimeters (which is

---

11. THE LEFT EYE. — *Analysis of the Colors of the Eye.* — The subject's face being turned toward the light, and his eyes fixed on those of the observer, the following points are to be noted:
   a) The color of the inner (central) circle. Pigment.
   b) "   "   " external (peripheric) circle.
   c) The possible confusion of the pigment (a) with an adjoining class.
   d) Peculiarities.
12. THE NOSE. — The following points are to be noted:
   a) The profile: Form of the Ridge: Base. Root.
   b) The dimension: Length. Projection. Breadth.
   c) Peculiarities.
13. THE FOREHEAD. — The inclination, apparent height and width, and peculiarities are noted.
14. MARKS AND SCARS. — The following points are to be noted.
   a) Nature and origin.
   b) Direction or inclination.
   c) Approximate dimensions.
   d) Accurate location with regard to specified points of the body.
   The plates accompanying the "instructions" give as near as possible, the correct position, and, in an abbreviated form, the manner in which measurements are taken.
   Follow strictly the "Instructions" not only as to measurements and general description, but also particularly as to marks, scars, etc., using abbreviations as found therein.

shown in the chapter relating to this measurement to be the largest possible divergency) a difference of four millimeters or more between two head-length measurements would be conclusive proof to him that the measurements were obtained from two different individuals.

19.   The conclusion in this instance would be the more forcible seeing the *examined subjects cannot exercise the slightest influence on their cranium diameters.*

20.   Quite frequently you may come across two subjects of the same height, the length of the head of one of them measuring 17 centimeters and a few millimeters; of the other 19 centimeters and more.   These individuals, whatever their other points of resemblance may be, cannot and must not be confounded with each other.

21.   On the other hand, when all the measurements and descriptive indications concur within the limits of possible errors or divergencies, the probability of identity becomes very great and almost equivalent to a certainty.

INSTRUCTIONS FOR TAKING DESCRIPTIONS.

(By Alphonse Bertillon).

PART FIRST.

ANTHROPOMETRIC INFORMATION.

CHAPTER I.

MEASURES TAKEN BY MEANS OF THE CALIPER-COMPASSES, (CRANIUM DIAMETERS).

SECTION I.

MEASURE OF THE LENGTH OF THE HEAD.

First Movement (Fig. 5.)

1. Seat the subject on a stool, face turned toward the light, but slightly inclined toward the floor.

2. Stand to the left of the subject, place the left point of the calipers in the cavity at the root of the nose,* holding the

---

* Note.—In anthropology, the point from which the antero-posterior diameter of the head is taken, is the glabella (space between eye-brows) and not the root of the nose. Hence, a difference of several millimeters between the scientific diameter of the anthropologist's system and the length of the head according to our way of measuring.

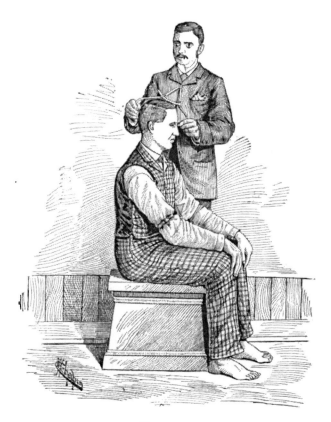

FIGURE 5.

LENGTH OF THE HEAD.

First Movement.

The operator places and maintains the end of the left branch in the cavity of the root of the nose; then, with eyes fixed on the graduation he moves the right extremity up and down the middle of the back of the head, until he finds the maximum point, and reads the indication.

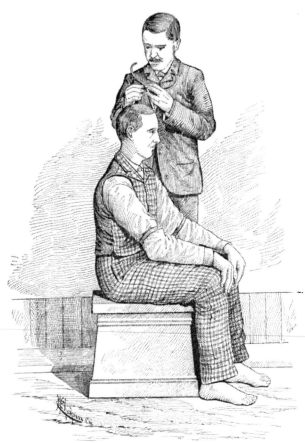

Figure 6.

LENGTH OF THE HEAD.

Second Movement. Fixing the set-screw at the surmised length on the graduation. (For position of fingers when behind the instrument, see Figure 8.)

Third Movement. For this movement the position is the same as in Figure 5.

rounded extremity of the point between thumb and forefinger, which rest on the adjoining parts of the nose and prevent the point from deviating, or entering either of the two orbital cavities.

3. At the same time, with your right hand take hold of the corresponding branch of the calipers and bring it toward the top and middle of the head, the extreme point to extend by one or two centimeters beyond the tips of the fingers, in order to easily penetrate the hair.

4. The other fingers, being slightly bent toward the palm, should hold the calipers in a semi-oblique position, in such a way that the light from the window strikes directly on the millimetric graduation.

5. Fix your eyes on the index of the graduation; move the right hand point of the calipers down the middle of the back of the head, until it reaches and goes beyond the maximum point; move the point of the compasses upward again, always taking care that it touches the scalp; pass over the maximum again, grope a few seconds, your eyes fixed on the graduation, so that you are very sure to strike the maximum point; finally read the indication on the graduation.

6. The maximum point is generally located on the occipital bone, sometimes a little above it. The operator must not forget, however, that he is not determining the location of this point, but rather the exact distance that separates it from the root of the nose.

Second Movement. (*Fig. 6.*)

7. The operator, having estimated within a few millimeters the length of the head, withdraws the calipers, and fastens the set-screw exactly at the surmised length on the graduation.

8. To do this latter movement rapidly and without fumbling:

9. Hold your fingers as indicated in Fig. 6, viz.: The left thumb across the left arm and the graduated scale of the calipers, the other fingers scarcely reaching the under part of the right arm. With the thumb and forefinger of the right

hand, move the right arm to the millimetric point obtained, and turn the set-screw on the reverse of the indicator.

10. In this movement the four outstretched fingers of the left hand serve as a guide, and prevent the oscillations which could not fail to appear if the right hand was acting alone.

11. *In fixing the calipers, see that the dart on the indicator is directly opposite the line of the ascertained measurement, and not at the side of it, half a millimeter either way.*

Third Movement.

12. Having set the caliper-compasses to the opening found, bring them back to the root of the subject's nose, and recommence the up and down motions described in the first movement. (See again Fig. 6.)

13. By these latter motions the operator checks the correctness of the obtained measurement, and tries to ascertain by oscillating the calipers whether or not the bony bump to the right or the left of the median line has escaped his attention at the first measurement, which would modify the maximum found. If the point at this operation encounters a resistance, the operator widens the opening on the caliper-compasses by one or two millimeters, handling the instrument as has been explained in the second movement.

14. If, on the other hand, the point touches no part, or if the friction on the maximum point is almost imperceptible, the operator narrows the opening by one or two millimeters. Very seldom after a few days' practice has he to resort to more than one or two gropings. Generally the measurement will be found correct at the first trial. *Still, be the operator ever so expert, he must never omit this third movement, which we call the movement of verification.*

15. In this verification the operator must particularly look out for the more or less distinguishable friction of the point on the scalp. The left point of the compasses resting closely on the root of the nose, the right point must *touch* the scalp; but it is not necessary, in order to pass the maximum point, to apply the least pressure on the arms, which unfortunately are elastic

enough to admit of straightening to a certain extent. When this occurs, it is a sure indication that the measurement is too small by one or two millimeters.

16. If the calipers are *fixed* to the exact dimension, the friction will become *null* when the opening is one millimeter wider, and *hard* when the opening is one millimeter narrower.

17. Thus the *measurement of the length of the head* obtained under the conditions and in the manner just explained, *is easily taken within one millimeter*. If two successive measurements of the same individual present a difference of two millimeters the operator *is at fault;* at *very great fault*, if this difference exceeds two millimeters. The error in this case would be so much more inexcusable as there is no trickery possible on the part of the subject as far as the head is concerned.

18. The interval of two millimeters is generally the result of a double mistake inversely made, of one millimeter each; the differences join each other, and the true finding lies between the two.

SECTION II.

MEASUREMENT OF THE WIDTH OF THE HEAD.

19. The greatest width of the head is taken with the same instrument as the length, and in a somewhat similar manner.

First Movement (Fig. 7.)

20. The subject being seated on the stool, in the same position as for length, station yourself directly behind him, your heels touching each other at right angles, your body erect, and your elbows evenly balanced and enjoying perfect freedom.

Take hold of the arms of the caliper compasses very near their extremities, and place the points against the skull, resting them upon the upper junction of the ears and head; then pressing them lightly against the scalp, and maintaining them on an even plane, slowly raise the instrument.

21. As was said in the length movement, the operator, keeping his eyes intently fixed on the graduation, will observe at first a widening movement quickly followed by a narrowing one, the latter continuing uninterruptedly until the top of the head is reached.

Descending with the instrument, the operator will notice that the reverse will be the case; and it should be his endeavor to find out by this feeling process the two points, directly opposite each other, on the same level, where the spread of the compasses is the greatest.

22. These points are not necessarily those of the greatest diameter, but they are situated very near it, and upon the same horizontal plane. The operator having thus found this horizontal plane has now only to:

23. Move his compasses slowly once or twice backward and forward until he is able to stop at the greatest measurement, and then read the graduation.

24. Sometimes the two points giving the greatest width are situated just where the upper part of the ear is joined to the head, but most frequently they are found a trifle to the rear of that locality, and a little higher up.

Second Movement (Fig. 8).

25. The second movement of the measurement of width has the same object as the corresponding movement of length, that of fixing the compasses at the measurement found by means of the set screw. There is this difference, however, that for the *width* it is preferable that the points of the compasses should remain on the two maximum points of the measurement, the opening being thus maintained, and the setting of the screw at the exact point facilitated.   .

26. While fixing the set screw, hold the compasses in the same manner as for "length," viz.: The left hand, relinquishing its grasp of the point and disengaging itself from the instrument, is carried toward the graduation bar, across which the thumb is placed, while the other fingers are extended beneath, in order to sustain and keep immovable the opposite

FIGURE 7.

WIDTH OF THE HEAD. ·

First Movement.

The operator with eyes fixed on the graduation ascertains the probable width to within a millimeter.

FIGURE 8.

WIDTH OF THE HEAD.

Second Movement.

Fixing the set screw at the surmised width without removing the instrument from the head.—Note the position of the fingers.

arm, which may now in its turn be abandoned by the right hand.

27. With this free hand turn the set-screw, after having assured yourself, however, that the spread of the arms has not varied during the manœuver.

Third Movement.

28. In the third movement, the compasses being set at the ascertained width, the operator satisfies himself that the opening is neither too wide nor too narrow.

29. To this end move the points of the compasses symmetrically up and down, gradually advancing a millimeter or two to the front with each up and down movement, until the bumps of the maximum width have been entirely cleared (same figure as for the first movement, Fig. 7).

30. During this verification it is very important that the subject should be squarely and firmly seated, and that the operator should stand perfectly erect, with elbows free and symmetrically raised, so that the points of the compasses may advance evenly.

31. The observations to be made regarding the degree of friction *and the approximation that it is possible to obtain*, are the same as for length.

32. A comparison, however, of the instructions for the third movement with those for the first, shows that the oscillating movements for verifying the probable width are not identical with those that determine it at the first reading of the measurement.

33. In *determining* the probable width, the compasses must first be raised vertically, then swung from front to rear; in *verifying*, the points (starting from the commencement of the third movement) advance from rear to front, but in describing a series of irregular up and down lines about two or three centimeters in length, and but a few millimeters apart. (Fig. 9, Sketch A.)

34. The bumps that determine the maximum width are often nothing more than slight protuberances, smaller in cir-

cumference than a ten cent piece. In these verifying oscillations, if the zig-zag lines are spread too far apart, there is great
danger of passing by the maximum bump without touching it,
(Fig. 9, Sketch B), and, in consequence, of being led to diminish the spread of the compasses, and to announce a measurement one or two millimeters two narrow.

35. Errors may be caused more easily still, if, in this verification movement, the points of the compasses are made to describe a series of concentric ovals (Fig. 9, Sketch C) instead
of following the zig-zag course laid down. This latter is a
very common fault with inexperienced operators.

OBSERVATIONS APPLICABLE TO THE MEASUREMENT OF BOTH
DIAMETERS.

36. Corrections and remarks, made necessary by any peculiarity in the indication of the length and width of the head,
are not frequent.

37. Sometimes a wound will cause a measurement to be
inexact, or may even render the operation for the time being
impossible. The observer, the better to shield himself from
responsibility, ought to be careful to note for reference all such
cases of ineffectual effort.

38. When a measurement seems extraordinary, either from
being excessively large or excessively small, it may be useful
to note by some common sign, that no mistake has been made
either by the operator or the recorder. In such cases it is better to write immediately after the dictated figures the letters
Rv. (abbreviation for reviewed, measurement reviewed, veri-
fied, the exactness of which is guaranteed, no matter how im-
probable it may appear.)

39. To mark a limit for extraordinary dimensions, let us
say, for example, that a head length beyond 20.5 or below 17
centimeters ought to be followed by the abbreviation "Rv."
The same may be said of head widths beyond 17 and below 14
centimeters.

40. The abbreviation "Rv" may appear with equal pro-
priety at the end of every other indication, whether in figures

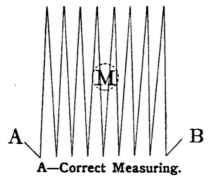

A—Correct Measuring.

A.—B. Course followed by one of the points of the compasses on the side of the head. Point M, centre of Maximum.

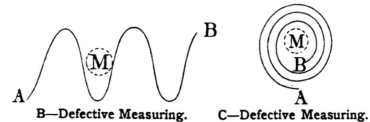

B—Defective Measuring.

A.—B. Course when the zigzag lines described by the compasses are too far apart. Point M, centre of Maximum, not touched by the compasses.

C—Defective Measuring.

A.—B. Circular course described by the compasses around point M, centre of Maximum, not touched by the compasses.

FIGURE 9.

WIDTH OF THE HEAD.

THIRD MOVEMENT.

For general position see Figure 7.   See text, § 33, 34 and 35.

or words. But it is for cranium diameters that it is more especially used.

41. Irregular or deformed heads should also be noted in the explanatory remarks, and especially so when these irregularities may lead to mistakes in measurement.

42. Non-symmetry in the cranium bumps that determine the greatest width should not lead the measurer to modify the manual of operation. He ought in such a case to observe with greater care than ever the *regularity* and *evenness* of his own movements while verifying, and should besides, note for reference the spread, necessarily less, obtained when the head is measured on any other than a regular diameter or axis. A note will explain these particulars, thus: Head irregular, (or very irregular) width inclining to the right (or left) side, measures only 14–5.

CHAPTER II.

MEASUREMENTS TAKEN BY MEANS OF THE SLIDING COMPASSES.

SECTION I.

MEASUREMENT OF THE LEFT MIDDLE FINGER.

1. The measurement of this finger is accomplished by means of the small branches of the sliding compasses. This indication is valuable for the reason that it can be *taken exactly, or to within about one millimeter.* It varies in individuals, be. sides, to the extent of more than 3 centimeters, and deception in connection with it is impossible. Although the measurement is a delicate one the operator in taking it is practically independent of the subject.

2. The indication to be ascertained is the length of the middle finger of the left hand measured from its extremity to the metacarpal joint, the finger being bent at right angles to the back of the hand. The operation may be divided into three movements.

First Movement (Figs. 10 and 11).

3. Plant the end of the large branch of the sliding-compasses obliquely against your chest; stand in front of the subject; grasp his left middle finger with your left hand, and place it on the back of the compasses, *taking care that the end of the middle finger rests firmly against the small stationary branch,* and that the subject's other fingers (forefinger, third and little fingers) extend past the shank on each side.

FIGURE 10.

LEFT MIDDLE FINGER.

1ST MOVEMENT.

The operator places the finger to be measured on the back of the compasses.

FIGURE 11.

LEFT MIDDLE FINGER.

Second Movement.

The operator turns one-quarter way around, raising the elbow at the same time, and brings the finger to be measured in a position at right angles to the back of the hand.

Third Movement.

The operator having placed the subject's hand in position pushes up the sliding branch and reads the indication.

4. The precaution of having the other fingers thrust forward facilitates to a great extent the execution of the following movements:

5. Press the subject's little finger firmly against the shank, placing your own fingers at the same time in the position shown in the photograph of this operation, viz.:

The operator's left thumb resting upon the first joint of the subject's middle finger to prevent it sliding off the shank, while the other fingers exert a pressure upon the back of the subject's hand, keeping it bent at right angles and forcing the extremity of the middle finger firmly against the heel of the small branch.*

6. With the right hand support the shank of the compasses a little below the sliding branch, grasping it in a way to enable you to push the latter forward a centimeter or two at will.

7. In this situation the middle finger is presented in an almost correct position.

Second Movement (*Fig.* 11.)

8. Turn your body one-quarter way around, retaining control of the hand of the subject, who must remain in his original position.

9. As a result of the change in your respective positions, the subject's arm is extended but half its length, and his wrist is slightly bent. In this position, in which the extensor tendons of the subject's hand are stretched to their utmost, and the flexor tendons of the palm of the hand contracted, there are but few middle fingers, be the hand ever so calloused, that cannot be made to take the rectangular position, however little the operator may aid the movement by keeping his thumb on the first joint of the subject's finger, and by exerting at the same time with his other fingers a pressure on the back of the subject's hand (Fig. 11, 2d).

---

* NOTE.—If the nail should protrude beyond the flesh of the finger the operator should pare it off with small scissors.

This pressure, we repeat, has the triple effect of forcing the end of the middle finger against the heel of the branch, of preventing the first joint from becoming detached from the shank, and of maintaining the finger in a position at right angles to the back of the hand.

10. The operator's movements should be easy, and he should keep his left shoulder elevated, to prevent the subject changing position or accompanying him in his quarter turn. (A comparison of the photographs of the first and second movements will make this clearer.)

Third Movement.

11. With rather a quick movement push forward the slide held by the right hand, press lightly, and read the graduation before freeing the subject's hand.

12. For *this measurement*, which should be as precise as that of the head, *the millimeter must be announced as carefully as the centimeter.* When the slide stops precisely at a half millimeter the operator will decide on the preceding or following millimeter, according as his judgment may dictate. In such a case, however, the measurement may be taken over again. A second trial will generally overcome the difficulty by showing the slide arrested nearer to one millimeter or the other.

13 *Above all things, in this measurement (and the caution is equally applicable to all the others) avoid giving "round numbers" or measurements terminating with fives, both indicative of carelessness, but set the instrument and announce exactly the figures it indicates.*

14. The practice of using round numbers or convenient figures approximating the true measurement, is but one more source of error in addition to those already pointed out.

FIGURE 11. 2D.

LEFT MIDDLE FINGER.

Enlargement of the position of the fingers in the third movement.

SECTION II.

MEASUREMENT OF THE LEFT LITTLE FINGER.

15. Proceed in this measurement in the same manner as in that of the middle finger.

16. The measurement of the little finger is more delicate than that of the middle finger. It is often difficult to detach the first joint of this finger from the corresponding and more prominent joint of the third finger, which has a tendency to join the former in pressing against the small branch of the instrument, thus increasing by one or two millimeters the measurement desired. To avoid this, take care always to press the subject's little finger against the back of the shank, and closely into the upper angle of the compasses, instead of midway between the two angles as in the middle finger measurement. To facilitate this manœuver and to accommodate the joint of the third finger, the corners of the branches have been hollowed out.

REMARKS APPLICABLE ALIKE TO THE MEASUREMENT OF THE MIDDLE AND LITTLE FINGERS.

Anchylosis (*Privation of the Movement of the Joints.*)

17. The principal observation to make relative to the measurement of the middle and little fingers refers to anchylosis, more or less complete, of the joints.

18. In cases of complete anchylosis it is necessary to distinguish between *rectilineal anchylosis*—which cannot alter the measurement—and *rectangular anchylosis*.

19. It is not necessary to speak of intermediate or obtuse-angled anchylosis, as it is very rarely met with.

20. When anchylosis forces the finger to remain completely bent (rectangular anchylosis) the figures of the measurement are but little greater than one could obtain by measuring the first joint by itself. It should be recorded as the

instrument indicates, and with it a note referring to the description of private marks, in some such form as this: "*Rectangular anchylosis of the joints*" (specifying by their names the joints so affected); and finally the measurement of the middle and little finger of the right hand should be added to the note.

21.   But the most frequent cause of error in the finger measurements is partial anchylosis, or rather a slight stiffening of the joints which, among laboring men (blacksmiths and handlers of the pick and shovel especially), prevents often a rectilineal extension of the fingers of the hand.

22.   You will proceed in such a case in the same way as for bent toes (see remark on the Foot chapter). The measure. ment of the left finger is taken as precisely as possible, and the result written down in its regular place, while the anchylosis is indicated by the letter " K " after the dictated figure, followed by the approximate number of millimeters by which this peculiarity might have shortened the actual length of the finger. These figures vary between 2, 3, 4 or 5 millimeters, seldom more.

23.   There is no necessity in such a case to give the meas-.urement of the corresponding finger of the right hand, as this kind of stiffening, when it appears at all, is generally common to both hands.

Partial or Total Amputation.

24.   If one or more joints of the two fingers to be measured are amputated, give the length of the remaining member, just as it is found, noting the following in "remarks":

1.   An explanation of the peculiarity.

2.   The length of the corresponding finger of the right hand.   For instance:

The two last phalanges of the left middle finger are amputated, right middle finger 12—3.

Exceptionally small lengths, caused sometimes by surgical operations, are indications too valuable in point of view of classification to be rejected when observed.

SECTION III.

MEASUREMENT OF THE LEFT FOOT.

25. Procure a solid firm bench, 30 centimeters wide, 50 centimeters long, and 40 centimeters high (which will also do for seating the subject for his head measurements).

Trace in the middle of the longer side of the surface of the bench, in a permanent way, the outlines of a left foot, indicating where the subject is to stand.

First Movement. (*Fig.* 12).

26. Have the subject take the position indicated by the photograph. In order to do this, follow closely the following directions, and have them minutely carried out:

Place the bench at a short distance from a point of support (a chair, corner of a table, or the like), elevated in proportion to the height of the subject; then give the order, "*Put your left foot on the tracing.*" This being done, "*Lean your body forward, and put your right hand on the chair (table corner or whatever it is),*" and then add, "*Stand on the bench on one foot.*"

28. By following the order and form of this direction, you will force the most stupid individual to put himself in regular position.

29. This position aims at forcing the subject to put the whole weight of his body on the left foot alone, which, being opposite to the right hand of the operator, is easier to measure than the right foot. By ordering the subject to lean his right hand on a point of support, the operator causes him to incline his body forward and to displace his center of gravity accordingly, a movement which naturally forces the toes to straighten automatically.

30. Before placing the instrument the operator must satisfy himself that the toes are in a natural position, and particularly that the big toe does not rest sideways on the bench, which would make it appear and measure smaller.

31. It is unnecessary to say that if it is bent either volun
tarily or involuntarily, the operator must himself rectify its
position by pressing it down with his fingers.

32. As a general thing when the big toe is bent intention-
ally the trick can be discovered by observing the position of
the other toes, which involuntarily follow the movement of the
big toe, and present at first glance a strikingly wrinkled skin.

33. It is difficult, however, for the subject to maintain this
false position longer than a minute. To restore the toe to its
normal position, it is generally sufficient to order the subject
to slightly bend the knee that supports the weight of the body.

34. After having ascertained the normal position of the
body, the foot, and particularly of the big toe, place your sliding compasses squarely against the foot in such a way that the
back of the heel rests closely with pressure against the stationary branch of the instrument, and the inner side of the heel
and the joint of the big toe touch the shank.

35. With very flat feet it happens frequently that the tar-
sus (reverse of the instep) instead of forming an arch forms a
protuberance underneath, and prevents the shank of the instrument from touching the inner side of the heel. In this case it
is sufficient to place the instrument against this protuberance
parallel to the position it would have occupied without this
anomaly.

36. Of whatever size the tarsal arch may be, do not hesitate to apply the instrument with *some pressure* against the heel
as well as against the side of the foot. The measurement will
be so much the more precise.

Second Movement (*Fig.* 13.)

37. Bring down the slide of the compasses with a light
movement, not as sharp as for the measurement of the fingers,
but still sharp enough to touch sufficiently.

38. Apply a pressure with your right thumb on the first
and second joints of the big toe, to make sure that the pushing
of the slide has not bent it, and that the subject has not volun-
tarily bent his toes. Then ask the subject to bend his left

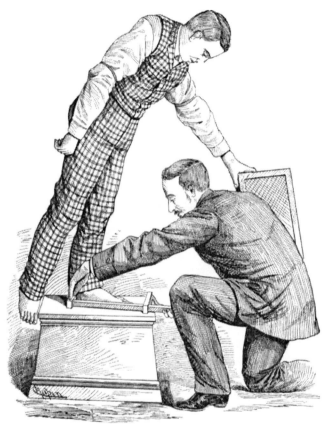

FIGURE 12.

LEFT FOOT

First Movement.

The operator having placed the subject in the position represented above, presses the stationary branch of the instrument firmly against the heel, taking care at same time that the shank touches the inner side of the heel as well as the joint of the big toe.

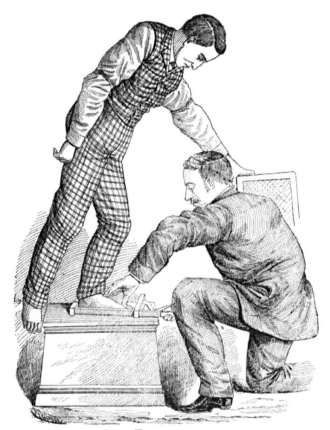

FIGURE 13.

LEFT FOOT.

Second and Third Movements.

The operator pushes forward the slide with the right hand, requests the subject to slightly bend the left knee, presses down the first and second joints of the big toe, sees that the other toes are not bent, rectifies if necessary the position of the instrument and reads the figures indicated knee, accompanying, if necessary, this command with a slight pressure on the inside of the knee.

39. The flexion of the knee and the pressure on the toe are ordinarily sufficient to straighten the foot. The slide will move back by itself, one or two millimeters, under the simple impetus of the straightened toe.

Third Movement.

40. Before reading, replace and lightly tighten the instrument which the movement of bending the knee may have disarranged; finally dictate the indicated figure.

41. Be careful when you press down the big toe, as above directed, not to apply the pressure on the extremity of the toe nail, which would cause the flesh to swell and unduly increase the length. Try simply to flatten the two joints.

42. Operators should avoid the reasoning which implies that a shoe made after a measurement so close and precise as ours could never be made to fit. Our object is not to make a pair of shoes, but to find the actual and unchangeable length of the foot, a length which may always be measured with absolute correctness, wherever and whenever it may be required.

43. The *limit of the approximation allowed for the measurement of the foot is one and in certain cases two millimeters*, which, taking into consideration the doubling up of errors (see note Chap. I, end of Sec. 1.) may cause a variance of three millimeters between two consecutive measurements of the same foot. Such discrepancies, while they cannot exactly be called blunders, are always more or less an indication of negligence on the part of the operator.

REMARKS WITH REFERENCE TO THE MEASUREMENT OF THE LEFT FOOT.

44. The observations derived from the measurements of the foot have a bearing on four principal points.

NOTE.—The shank of the compasses should be kept clean, and oiled if necessary, in order to insure the free movement of the slide.

I. *Deviation of the big toe.*

45. The letter "d" following the figures indicating the measure of the foot, means that the big toe has deviated inward toward the other toes.

46. Mark down, after the initial, the number of millimeters by which this deviation is estimated as having diminished the measurement of the foot, for instance: Foot 24.6–d 3 means a foot 24 centimeters 6 millimeters, which at a former time before the toe had deviated would likely have measured 24 centimeters 9 millimeters.

II. *Contraction of the big toe.*

47. The letter "b" (abbreviation for bent),—" pl," *plie* in the French original—followed by the figures 2, 3, 4 (millimeters understood), corrects approximately the diminution caused by an habitual contraction of the big toe.

48. This deformity, generally caused by the wearing of too short shoes, is called, if it is very pronounced, by the characteristic name "*hammer shaped toe*," but it is seldom found as bad as that on the big toe. It would cause a diminution in the length of the foot not exceeding perhaps half a centimeter.

49. We cannot too strongly recommend that operators, by ordering the knee bent, and by applying a pressure on the first joint of the big toe, should ascertain, before making use of the abbreviation "b," that the contraction is not feigned or exaggerated.

III. *Projection of the second toe beyond the big toe.*

50. The third indication to be noted in connection with the measurement of the foot has reference to cases where the second toe projects beyond the big toe. This peculiarity is indicated by means of the sign $>$ used in mathematics to express inequality, which sign is to be preceded by the Roman figure II (understood as second toe) and followed by the number of millimeters by which the second toe extends past the first toe. For example: Foot 26.4–II$>$ 2, 3, or 4 millimeters.

51. This peculiarity of the second toe does not in any way change the manual of operation in measuring the foot.

52. The operator must not, in measuring, press back the second toe, but must take care that the sliding branch of the compasses touches the end of the foot, and that the flexion of the knee—*more particularly in cases of this kind*—is well executed.

53. The notation II >, besides constituting a particular mark for itself, calls attention to a slight source of mistake, which, if unperceived at a former measurement, might have rendered that measurement faulty.

IV. Amputation in whole or in part of the left foot.

54. As regards amputation of the foot, distinction must be made between total and partial amputation.

55. If the amputation is total, the measurement of the left foot takes its ordinary place under the indication "ooo" reference to particular marks, giving the following explanation:
   1. Description of the peculiarity.
   2. The length of the right foot in the following form:
      Foot (left) amputated above the ankle, right foot=20.4.

56. Proceed in a similar way, in case of partial amputation of the toes or of the entire front part of the foot, excepting that in this instance the measurement of the foot is to be given exactly as the instrument indicates it.

57. It is needless to state that in a case of this kind the rigorous precision of an ordinary measurement is out of place. The bending of the left knee, the pressure of the instruments, etc., need not be observed. Frequently the measurement has to be taken with the subject in a sitting position.

58. When the cicatrization is fresh, any measurement —even an approximate one—is postponed. Reference to "remarks" will give the explanation of such exceptional cases, and will shield the operator from responsibility.

SECTION IV.

MEASUREMENT OF THE LEFT FORE ARM.

59. . Use a rather high table and sliding compasses with a shank from 55 to 60 centimeters long. Have the subject take the following position :

First Movement (Fig. 14.)

60. The left fore arm and hand to form as acute an angle as possible with the arm, and rest flatly (finger nails up) on the edge of the table nearest the subject.

61. In this position, the protruding extremity of the elbow, the middle of the back surface of the wrist and the first joint and tip of the middle finger, must be in a straight line.

62. The arm must be very near the edge of the table, allowing the forefinger to rest directly on the very edge, and the thumb, detached from the other fingers, to hang on the side.

Second Movement.

63. Place the stationary branch of the sliding compasses against the elbow, the graded shank touching the fore arm and hand of the subject on the side of the little finger in a line parallel with the axis of the arm.

Third Movement. (Fig. 15.)

64. Bring down the sliding branch of the compasses until you touch, by slight pressure, the extremity of the middle finger ; then press down the hand and wrist of the subject, taking care that the entire forearm rests at full length on the table, and that the stationary branch still touches the point of the elbow.

65. Read and dictate the indication on the instrument.

REMARKS WITH REFERENCE TO THE MEASUREMENT OF THE FOREARM.

66. A portion of the observations in connection with the

FIGURE 14.

LEFT FORE-ARM.

First and Second Movements.

The operator places the subject in the position represented above, and presses the stationary branch closely against the point of the elbow, keeping the shank parallel to the axis of the arm.

FIGURE 15.

LEFT FORE-ARM.

Third Movement.

The operator pushes forward the sliding branch, presses lightly on the back of the subject's hand and wrist, satisfies himself that the roint of the elbow and the middle of the wrist are in line with the first joint and tip of the middle finger, and then reads the indicated measurement.

measurements of the forearm has already been given while explaining the measurement of the middle finger. It is unnecessary to repeat it here (anchylosis, stiffness of joints, amputation of the finger, etc.)

67. Beyond these cases, the obstacle most frequently occurring in connection with this measurement is the anchylosis, more or less complete, of the elbow. In such an event do as has been previously directed in the measurement of the foot, middle finger, etc., viz.: Measure the member as you find it, and give the exact length of the corresponding member on the opposite side.

68. The length of the forearm may, to a certain extent, be influenced by trickery, be it by moderately bending the fingers, or by exaggerating the natural cambering of the wrist.

68. Every time an attempt of this kind is suspected, mark down after the figures indicating the measurement, the letters "tr," (abbreviation for trickery), followed by the number of millimeters supposed to have thus been lost.

70. *The tolerated approximation for the measurement of the forearm is three millimeters* UNDER *and one millimeter only* ABOVE, *the correct figures.*

SECTION V.

MEASUREMENT OF THE RIGHT EAR.*

71. We add the measurement of the ear to the indications taken with the sliding compasses, although in practice this latter measurement is taken by means of compasses exclusively reserved for that purpose, of smaller size, but identical in form with the others (Fig. 3.)

---

* NOTE.—The right is to be measured in preference to the left ear (contrary to our preference as to other measurements) because it is more accessible to the operator, also on account of the prevailing custom in photography to take the right profile in preference to the left.

72. Generally you proceed with this measurement after taking those of the length and width of the head; that is to say before using the large sliding compasses, at a moment when the subject is standing erect. Operators of small stature, however, prefer to take this measurement when the subject is yet seated.

First Movement (*Fig.* 16.)

73. The subject, his face turned toward the window, is told to slightly incline his head to the left, and backward, so as to present the ear in full view, and allow the lower end of the shank of the compasses to drop below the shoulder.

74. With your right hand place the shank of the compasses in a nearly vertical position, parallel with the line determined by the " tragus " and the upper and nether attachments of the ear, the shorter ends of the branches of the compasses toward the back of the head, and as flat as possible against the skull, the stationary branch above, the sliding branch below.

Second Movement.

75. With your left hand hold fast and immovable the stationary branch of the compasses, by taking as a point of support the top of the subject's head. The thumb, lightly stretched, should rest firmly on the button of the branch, causing the latter to touch, *without depressing*, the upper rim of the ear. At the same time push with your right thumb the sliding branch, slowly, *flush* to the extreme point of the lobe of the ear.

76. In this movement, which requires very steady hands, it is better to put your right thumb on the pushing knob of the sliding branch.

Third Movement.

77. Read and dictate the indication of the compasses after having carefully glanced once more at the position of the two branches.

FIGURE 16.
RIGHT EAR.

FIRST MOVEMENT.—The operator gently touches the upper rim of the ear with the stationary branch, keeping it immovable by pressing the upper extremity firmly against the head with his left thumb, his fingers resting on the top of the subject's head.

SECOND MOVEMENT.—The shank of the compasses bring in a position parallel to the axis of the ear; the operator pushes forward the sliding branch until it touches very lightly the lowest point of the lobe. He then satisfies himself that the bell of the ear has not been compressed by the instrument, and reads the indication.

REMARKS WITH REFERENCE TO THE MEASUREMENT OF THE EAR.

78. We cannot too strongly recommend the exercise of caution in this operation, to avoid depressing the skin of the upper seam and of the lobe of the ear, which would easily cause a diminution of several millimeters.

79. Another difficulty presents itself in the lobe closely adhering to and extending along the cheek. In this case the measurement must be taken from the extreme end of the lobe, wherever that is.

80. This peculiarity, which may be a source of error, is indicated by the letters " pr," (prolonged) following the figures of the measurement.

81. Ears which are torn, cut or indented must be measured as they are, in accordance with the principles explained in the articles " Foot " and " Finger."

82. *The approximation tolerated for the measurement of the ear is one millimeter.*

44

CHAPTER III.

MEASUREMENTS TAKEN BY MEANS OF THE VERTICAL AND HORIZONTAL GRADUATED MEASURES.

SECTION I.

MEASUREMENT OF THE FIGURE (HEIGHT.)

1. In taking the height, the subject should be barefooted and standing in the position of a soldier, as it is defined in military tactics; the heels joined and touching the foot of the measure, the feet in a little more acute than rectangular position and turned symmetrically outward, the knees stretched, the body straight and plumb, shoulders back, and of even height, the arms hanging naturally along the body, the chin drawn slightly inward, the eyes looking straight ahead. (Fig. 17.)

2. With stoop-shouldered persons it results frequently from the above positions, that the back of the head does not touch the vertical rule of the graduated measure. It would be wrong to have such subjects lift their head until it touches the measure, and would likely cause a diminution of one centimeter from the real height.

3. As a general rule, let the subject stand so as to give his maximum height, taking care always that his heels touch the floor.

4. Of all the measurements, that of the stature is the most delicate, and the one in which, more than in any other, the subject can cheat. The least negligence in the above described

FIGURE 17.

THE HEIGHT.

(The subject being barefooted.)

position can change the actual figures by a centimeter. More-over, the body settles each year after twenty-five years of age, sometimes sooner. Supposing all these errors appear jointly, it may be taken for granted that an adult subject, whose body has been gradually settling during the several years inter-vening between two measurements may show a diminution of height to the extent of three centimeters, or an increase up to one centimeter.

5. Setting aside these natural causes, *the operator is at fault when there is a divergency of more than one centimeter, and at great fault where the divergency is more than two centimeters.*

6. Dictate the height by giving the centimeters exactly, and the millimeters approximately, as the graded measure may reveal them.

REMARKS WITH REFERENCE TO THE MEASUREMENT OF THE FIGURE.

7. Note down next to the space reserved for the indication of the height the estimated extent of the stoop of the back, if any, viz.: "st." 1, 2 or 3 centimeters. Where the position is correct and straight, which is oftenest the case, let the figure of the height be followed by St. with inverted commas, thus, " St."

8. By this correction the operator increases the reliability of the operation. He marks 1 centimeter when the individual is slightly stooped, 2 centimeters when the stoop is more pro-nounced, 3 centimeters when it is very pronounced. The figure 4 is only exceptionally used ; 5, 6, etc., apply to regular hunchbacks only.

9. The operator, by experimenting on himself before a measuring board and observing what diminution is produced by more or less stooping, will soon be able to estimate closely how much the measurement is diminished by the same defect in others.

10. Thus the notation : Height, 1 m, 65 St. 3 is applied to a man whose height by actual and correct measurement is 1 meter 65 centimeters, but who, under different circumstances,

when he was young or in good health, when he stood erect, or wanted to stand erect, would have measured 3 centimeters more, viz.: 1 meter 68 centimeters.

11. Again, the notation " height 1 m, 68 'St.'" (St. with inverted commas) is applied to a man standing fairly erect and straight, who, if all other indications agree, may be the same man described in the preceding paragraph.

SECTION II.

MEASUREMENT OF OUTSTRETCHED ARMS.

12. The measurement of the outstretched arms is the maximum length reached by the arms when stretched in the form of a cross with the body.

13. This measurement is taken by means of a wooden rule, two meters long, placed at the height of the shoulders on the back of the subject, who stretches his arms, at the same time slightly spreading his legs.

14. For permanent use trace on a plain flat wall a horizontal centimetric graduation, commencing at a meter from the starting point and continuing for two meters.

15. Trace the graduation at the height of the shoulders of an average man and extend it above and below, at least 20 centimeters wide, in order to suit any height. (Fig. 18.)

16. *The measurement of the outstretched arms is taken and dictated only in centimeters, the supplementary millimeters being always omitted.* The figure announced is, therefore, frequently 3, 4, or 5 millimeters below the actual length. When more than five millimeters, dictate the next following centimetric unity.

REMARKS WITH REFERENCE TO THE MEASUREMENT OF THE OUTSTRETCHED ARMS.

17. It is certainly unnecessary to note the millimeters in a

FIGURE 18.

THE OUTSTRETCHED ARMS.

The measurement from finger tip to finger tip, the arms being extended in a right angular cross with the body.

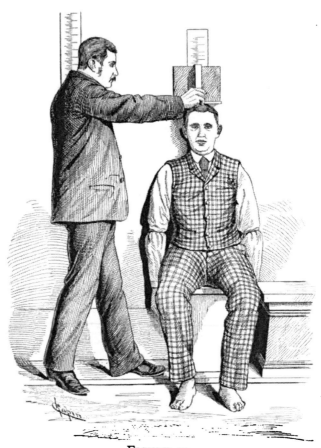

FIGURE 19.

MEASUREMENT OF THE TRUNK.

Seat the subject well back on the bench and closely against the wall, and see that he holds his body erect.

measurement where the subject can cheat to the extent of two centimeters above and three centimeters below the true figure.

18. Errors may be prevented by indicating the shrinking, from natural causes or otherwise, of the length of the out-stretched arms, in a similar way as in the height.

19. This correction has frequently to be made with persons who have the joints of their arms stiffened from rheumatism, rachitis, etc.

20. If a person insists that he is not able to spread and stretch his arms, it is not in the line of duty of the operator to discover whether or not the inability really exists. He measures the longest tension of the arms as he finds it, even if by laxation or paralysis of either of the arms, the measurement should be reduced to the length of one arm only, added to the width of the shoulders. But he must in an explanatory note carefully mark down the *probable* length, which would be revealed if both arms could be freely and fully stretched.

21. With those who are afflicted with rachitis (inflammation of the spine) care must be taken that their wrists press as closely as possible against the graduation on the wall. If necessary, assist this movement by a light pressure of the joint.

22. From the point of view of identification the measurement of the outstretched arms is of only secondary importance. It does not follow however that in this measurement the operator may remit the attention and care, which, under all circumstances should be given to every detail of his work.

SECTION III.

MEASUREMENT OF THE TRUNK.

23. Procure for this special purpose a bench 25 centimeters wide, 30 centimeters long, and 40 centimeters high, and fasten it lengthwise squarely against the wall.

24. Place on the wall a graduated measure, about 1 meter 20 centimeters long, *starting from the surface of the bench.*

First Movement (Fig. 19.)

25. The subject, being in shirt sleeves, is told to sit on the bench, " your buttocks close to the wall." Ascertain by passing the hand down the back of the subject if this order is strictly complied with, and convince yourself that the small of the back is thrust against the wall, the shoulders evenly sloping, and the head in its normal position.

Second Movement.

26. Bring down the measuring square (same as for measurement of the figure) and dictate the figures indicated.

REMARKS WITH REFERENCE TO THE MEASUREMENT OF THE TRUNK.

27. The points to be observed in connection with the shrinking or the contracting of the back, or with possible trickeries are the same as explained with reference to the stature and outstretched arms, and must be corrected in a similar way.

28. The measurement of the trunk varies upwards of 10 centimeters on individuals of the same length of figure, and is easily taken correctly within 3 or 4 millimeters on willing subjects. *The difference between two measurements of the same subject*, whatever the cause of errors may be, *ought never to exceed* 1 *centimeter;* taking into consideration of course, the corrections indicated by the shrinkage of the trunk.

FIGURE 20.
LEFT EYE.

The observer turns his back to the light, invites the subject to look him straight in the eye, and notes the color or shade of pigment of the left eye.

PART SECOND.

CHAPTER I.

NOTATION OF THE COLOR OF THE EYES.

GENERAL PRINCIPLES.

1. The prevalent confusion in designating the color of the eye arises largely from the necessity one is put to, while taking descriptions so called, to ascertain the color of the iris under different lights. Thus, for instance, a dark blue eye turned from the light, observed at a distance of several meters, appears black, owing to the contrast of the dark colored iris with what is commonly called the white of the eye.

2. The so-called *"gray"* eye, is generally nothing but a blue eye with a more or less yellowish tint, appearing gray on account of the shadow cast by the eyebrows.

3. All other qualificatives in use for designating the color of the eyes participate in this confusion, and must be left out of the reader's consideration.

4. In analyzing in a uniform way the color of the iris the examiner should stand opposite his subject, at a distance of about 30 centimeters, his back to the light so that the eye to be examined is struck by a full strong light (not the rays of the sun, however.) Then he orders the subject to look him straight in the eye, and lifts lightly with his right hand the middle of the subject's eyelid. (*Fig.* 20.)

50

5. It sometimes happens that the iris, observed in that way, presents notable differences in color and shade between the right and left eye. It is recommended however, that the observation be based exclusively on the left eye, which faces the right of the operator, the only exception being when the left eye has been permanently injured, or is wanting.

6. The examiner must not write down any observations until he has closely studied the eyes of a certain number of individuals, and become perfectly familiar with the principles of the system of notations hereinafter explained.

7. The eyeball consists of a central circle, called "*pupil*," and a colored circular band, called "*iris*."

8. Speaking of the color of the eye, it is the iris that is meant, the pupil always being black in the lightest as well as the darkest eyes.

9. In the iris two principal zones are distinguished: 1. The *central* or *pupillary zone* sometimes called "*areola*," or small circle, or *circle* simply. (It borders the pupil.) 2. The *peripheric or external* zone (the part of the iris next to the white of the eye.)

10. Our notation is based on the theory that there is found in the human race but two fundamental types of eyes, the *blue* eyes and the *maroon* eyes. All other shades must be considered as intermediate between these two types.

11. We understand by *blue*, or better expressed, *impigmented* eyes (absence of pigment.—See § 14.) the pale blue, azure blue, violet blue and slate blue eyes. We may add that these subdivisions are frequently difficult to define. Many eyes of more or less bluish tint may participate in two or three of these qualificatives at once, Fig. 21 (A to F.)

12. The *maroon* eyes have a unique tint, which reminds one of the shell of the *marron* (French chestnut) or of a horse chestnut when the fruit is ripe and fresh, and the shell sleek and shining. It is the " black" eye, the eye of the Arab, the negro, and of people from southern climes generally. The shade of this eye is more or less deep, more or less light, but its gen-

eral aspect is more uniform than that of the series of blue eyes.*

13. The intermediate eyes, to which class three-fourths of the eyes of the Caucasian race belong, generally approach either the impigmented eye (pale, azure, violet or slate blue) or the maroon eye. The delicacy or the intensity of their pigmentation is the basis of their denomination and subsequent classification.

PIGMENT.

14. By *pigment of the eye* we mean the more or less yellowish-orange colored matter which is observed in most eyes, when they are examined under the conditions of light given at the beginning of this chapter (§ 4). The more abundant this pigment is in the eye, the darker it appears, and the nearer it approaches the maroon.

15. In most cases this yellowish-orange colored matter is collected in the shape of a circle or areola around the pupil, and sometimes appears in little dots or small triangular spots in the external zone.

16. The four varieties of pigmentation, which serve for the notation and classification of intermediate eyes, are yellow, orange, hazel and maroon.

17. Eyes of an imperfect maroon color, in other words, those whose surface is not entirely covered with maroon, are subdivided as follows: 1. *Maroon circle*, where the maroon is grouped around the pupil. 2. *Irisated maroon*, where the pigment enters a portion of the external zone, and leaves exposed on the surface of the iris only small triangular or crescent shaped spots, either of greenish yellow or of dark slate-blue color.

---

* NOTE.—It has been suggested to substitute a more suitable word for the qualificative *Maroon*, which as ordinarily understood, describes a tint of a dark claret color, (more reddish than the color of the iris, we intend to describe by Maroon.) We have decided, however, to retain the qualificative MAROON, with the understanding that in connection with the description of the eye, it means exactly what the word ought to indicate, viz.: *The color of a marron (French chestnut)*, or what will be better understood in the United States, *the color of a horse chestnut*, (see also page 52, § 23 (3) and page 57 § 44.]

18. This distinction between *circle* and *irisated* is also applicable to other pigmentations, but as a descriptive information only, without calling for subdivisions.

19. To resume : The subdivisions finally obtained appear in the following classification, in which a place is found for eyes of every description :

    1. Impigmented (that is, the iris is entirely without the yellowish-orange matter.)
    2. Pigmented yellow.
    3.   "   orange.
    4.   "   hazel (incompletely.)
    5.   "   maroon in circle. } (See § 17).
    6.   "   "   irisated.
    7.   "   pure maroon.

This scale of colors must be committed to memory, and the meaning of the expressions perfectly understood.

20. The yellow pigment is very like the color of pulverized sulphur (pale yellow.)

21. The orange is not exactly the color of the peel of that fruit but rather what the painter calls yellow ochre.

22. The hazel resembles burnt sienna, or the shell of a dry dusty hazel nut.

23. In practice, in the absence of a comparative scale, the varieties of pigmentation of the eye are classified by carefully observing the following distinctions :

    1. The yellow is distinguished from the orange by the manifest absence of reddish tints, or by a very scant pigmentation.
    2. The orange from the hazel by a more vivid shade, not tarnished with black.
    3. The maroon is distinguished from the hazel by a more velvety. more abundant and deeper pigmentation.

EXTERNAL ZONE. (PERIPHERIC.)

24. To complete the picture of the eye, mark on the second line directly under the pigmentation, the shade or tint of the

4

external zone (see § 9), without reference to the pigmentary irisations that may be found there. For that purpose employ expressions in common use. The adjectives mostly used for the first three classes are: Blue (followed or preceded by the qualificative pale, azure or slate), or else greenish blue, turbid blue, violet blue. *Never use the word gray*, which defines nothing, and only leads to misunderstandings.

25. The periphery of the " maroon circle" and " maroon irisated " pigmentations, is generally, as has been said before, light greenish-yellow, slate-blue-greenish, or dark greenish.

26. The periphery of "hazel" pigmented eyes will be found to have either the same shading as the next preceding or the next following tint in the pigmentary scale. It is generally greenish yellow, more or less dark, and often of a greenish blue.

USE OF THE WORDS "FRANK" AND "LIMITED."

27. In the notation of the color of the eye, the *indication of the pigment* is the *key to the classification;* an error on that point may make all future researches useless.

28. When you hesitate between two qualificatives, write on the *first* line the description seeming to you the most appropriate, and on the *third* (the second line being reserved for the indication of the periphery), the one in which a confusion may be possible, preceding this latter notation by the word " limited."

For instance, the formula:

Circle, orange medium,
Greenish-blue (light)
Limited circle yellow,

expresses a pigmentation intermediate between the yellow and the orange; that is, of a tint where the reddish is present in such small quantity, that it might escape the attention of another examiner. The nearest equivalent to an eye, " orange-limited yellow " is the eye " yellow-limited orange."

Again, an eye:

Maroon, pure medium,

"   "   "

Limited greenish maroon,

would designate a maroon eye, on which a close examination may discover greenish lines in a very small quantity, but sufficiently conspicuous to make it possible for another operator to classify the eye as follows:

Maroon, medium,

Greenish medium,

Limited maroon, pure.

29. Experience demonstrates that it is possible for an observer who is in the least familiar with the classification given above (§ 9) to hesitate between more than two qualificatives, or, which amounts to the same, to skip over an entire shade and classify as yellow, for instance, what he has classified as hazel before, or confound "orange" with "maroon," or "maroon circle" with an "eye, maroon pure."*

His hesitation and mistakes are necessarily limited to two neighboring indications. The limit is of great help in all doubtful cases. It is a safeguard, a hole to creep out of, which the operator cautiously keeps in readiness for himself.

30. Where there is no cause for hesitation at all, indicate the absence of the limit by writing down on the third line the word "frank." For instance:

Yellowish blue

"   "

Frank.

TONE AND COMPLEMENTAL SIGNS.

31. Besides the designation of component colors, the following must be specified:

1. The tone or intensity of these colors
2. Their respective quantities.

---

* Note.—The only exception to this rule is the hazel pigmentation, which may be limited by "circle maroon" and by "maroon greenish." (See § 43.)

32. The intensity of the color or shade is expressed by the following words: Light, medium, deep.

Thus, an eye described as "deep yellow, blue azure medium" indicates an eye of ordinary blue, irisated with deep yellow, that is, a pronounced yellow; while "light yellow" would designate a pigmentation of the color of a lemon or pulverized sulphur.

33. The qualificative "*pale*," in conjunction with *blue*, means to express the presence of *whitish lines*, which must not be confounded with yellowish lines.

34. The quantity of a color is a descriptive element of no less importance than its intensity. When one of the elements is manifestly more prominent than the other, this prominence is marked by underlining the corresponding term. If, on the contrary, the subordinate shade of the general coloring of the iris, needs to be marked as against a more prominent shade, do it by means of parentheses ( ).

35. Thus an eye, "(light yellow) blue violet medium," indicates a blue eye irisated by feeble yellow lines; while an eye, "yellow (blue violet)" would apply to an eye in which the blue is, to say, merged. "Yellow (blue) and "yellow blue" are nearly equivalent; the former indication shows the presence of blue in smallest quantity, the other, the preponderance only of yellow.

36. When the shades constituting the coloring of the iris occupy on its surface approximately equal spaces, and when there is no occasion to underline one term in preference to the other, you express this equality by the sign — written on the third line before the words limited or frank.

37. Thus, just as the designation of each eye must, on the third line, be supplemented by the word frank or limited, each shade of color (besides the words "light," "medium" or "deep") must also be qualified by either an underlineation, by parenthesis ( ), or by the mathematical sign of equality —.

REMARKS ON A FEW EXCEPTIONAL CASES.

38. In most cases the intensity of the tint becomes greater,

the lower down the tint itself appears in the scale of colors. Thus, in describing the pigment, the "yellow" is most frequently to be inclosed by parentheses; the "orange," only once in a while; the "hazel" never.

39. Again, when you find an eye evidently blue, with only a few dots of a light and bright orange color (marigold color for instance) it is better to classify such an eye with the yellow, *i. e.*, the least pigmented, than with the orange. The same is the case :

(1). With the maroon circles, when narrow and scant; which are better classified as "hazel," that being the pigmentation nearer to them in quantity.

(2). With dark reddish circles when irregular and incomplete; which are classified with the "orange," in preference to the "hazel." In other words, the classification is based on the quality as well as on the quantity of the pigment. Where, in exceptional cases, the second factor does not correspond with the first, the eye retrogrades by one class, *i. e.*, is put in the next preceding class.

40. Let us say here once more, that the observer must, on such occasions, more particularly shield himself by giving the indication of possible limits

41. The hazel gives occasion for another observation of the same kind. From its place in the scale this class occupies the middle between the blue and the maroon eye, and contains only eyes of imperfect pigmentation. The result is, that it is preferable to rank as "maroon-greenish, limited hazel" eyes which are almost entirely of a deep hazel color, where the coloring matter is not collected as a circle around the pupil, but is indistinctly, though abundantly, spread all over the eye. The general aspect of such eyes is, however, much nearer the "maroon-greenish" than the "hazel circle."

---

*NOTE.—If it were not for this exception there would be eyes marked "limited-impigmented" in the division "orange," and vice versa, eyes marked "limited, orange" in the division of impigmented eyes. This skipping over an entire class (yellow) would disturb the classification. Besides, the orange in such small quantities is hard to distinguish from the yellow.

42., Regarding eyes " pigmented hazel pure " which by analogy, ought to be classified " maroon pure "—they are hardly ever found without some greenish mixture.

43. As an exception to the rule laid down in § 29, it must yet be remarked that the " hazel pigment " may be limited by both the 5th and the 6th divisions at the same time, and vice versa. This anomaly arises from the fact that the maroon is subdivided into three classes, while the other pigments, the yellow, orange and the hazel, form each a single class for themselves.

RECAPITULATION AND COMPARISON OF THE NEW NOTATION
WITH THE OLD ONE.

44. The maroon eye, whatever its shade may be, is defined by its name, and reminds you of the gradually darkening shades through which the shell of a "marron" or horse chestnut passes in its evolution toward maturity.

45. The azure blue is known by everybody. The turbid blue, or murky blue, is intermediate between the azure and slate blue.

The slate blue (or murky violet blue for the lighter shades) takes the place, in some cases, of the " gray blue " or the " gray."

46. No term is more vague or indefinite than the qualificative "*gray*," applied in ordinary practice to more than three-fourths of the descriptions taken. Properly speaking, the " gray " is a mixture of white and black, its complete scale extending from the black down to the white. As a specimen of gray, you might mention the spots left on white paper by a drawing stump over black crayon, or a dilution of India ink on white ground. Never will human eye, observed under prescribed conditions, present similar tints. The center of the eye, or pupil, is, as above stated, a small circle always black; as far as the iris is concerned, it has always a colored background and therefore cannot be qualified as gray. Looked at from a short distance and under good light, the gray eyes of the general public are " blue," " light yellowish," or

"pale purple-blue." It would seem then, that they belong always to the lighter tints, but by an inexplicable contradiction the general public applies the qualificative "gray " also to certain eyes of a dark blue hue, often called steel gray, eyes which we designate by the terms "slate-blue" for the darker shades, and " violet-blue" for the lighter shades. Everybody knows the color of common slate, while the bluish color of tempered steel is very vague, and hardly discernible.

47. The word gray is only good to produce confusion, and must never be used to designate the color of the eye.

48. The black eyes also require a few words of explanation. There is no more a black iris than a gray one. The eyes improperly black are generally of a deep maroon, sometimes of a dark slate-blue.

49. The expression "brown" is also applied to eyes, which we designate by " maroon medium," or " deep maroon," the same eyes that other people call " black."

50. *Pale* or *Turbid* (murky) can hardly be applied to any other than the blue eyes.

51. The qualificative " trouted" applicable to blue as well as maroon eyes, is used to designate certain red spots, also called fire spots, which resemble the speckles on the trout. These spots, frequently the result of a former disease of the iris, will not modify the classification of the eye, nor will they interfere with its denomination except as a special mark. Thus, the " slate-blue eye, trouted," or the " azure blue eye, trouted," are classified with the impigmented eyes, as long as the iris outside of their spots does not show any yellow matter. Other special marks of the eye are noted in the place for remarks at the foot of the descriptive list.

52. When the color of the left eye, for instance, differs from the color of the right, note the color of the left in its proper place, and the color of the right in the " remarks." The same with notations like the following: " Light or bad film on the right (or left) eye," etc., " squint eyed in the right (or left) eye," etc., etc.

With one eyed persons, make distinction between those who

are simply deprived of sight of one eye, and those that have the socket empty. Mark: "*Cannot see with the right (or left) eye*," for the former. "*Has the right (or left) eye put out or enucleated*," for the latter. If the subject wears a glass eye, make a note of that also.

ABBREVIATIONS—FORMULAE FOR THE EYES.

53. The space on the descriptive cards for the description of the eye being rather limited, it has been found necessary to adopt the following abbreviations, the use of which is obligatory.

blue	bl.	irisated	(see note).*
violet (purple)	viol.	circle	.C.
slate	sl.	concentric circle	C. c.
impigmented	imp.	light	l.
yellow	y.	medium	m.
orange	or.	deep or dark	d.
hazel	haz.	limited	lim.
maroon	mar.	frank	fr.
greenish	gr.		

54. In most cases the description of the eye occupies three lines:

    1. Pigmentation (circle or irisated.)
    2. External zone (without reference to pigmentation.)
    3. The word frank or limited (the latter giving the

NOTE.—The word irisated is very seldom used, three-fourths of the pigmentations being deposited right around the pupil, either in concentric circles, or in radiating or scalloped circles. Therefore the absence of the word circle (C) before a description of the pigment, implies the term irisated, more particularly, in notations of the maroon eye. The circle is called concentric when the not very abundant colored matter around the pupil is confined to a circular zone about one millimeter wide, as if cut out with a punch.

The "scalloped circle" is characterized by indentures and scallops of the pigment, reaching into the middle part of the iris.

In the radiating circle, the colored matter spreads over the entire concentric zone and from there seems to emit pigmentary rays into the external zone. This is the only group of hazel and maroon pigmentations.

The distinction between radiating and scalloped circle has nothing to do with the notation of the color of the eye. Only the concentric circle is noted by the abbreviation as shown above [Cc.]

possible confusion with tints other than that described in first line.)

55. The only exceptions to this rule are made with the impigmented (1st class) and the maroon pure eyes (7th or last class.) For the former, the line of pigmentation (1) is left blank. To indicate that this absence of a notation does not arise from error, put two quotation marks in lieu of the word impigmented. Thus:

                   ,,   ,,   ,,   ,,   ,,

Slate-blue medium,   *or* sl. bl. m.
Limited yellow,   lim. y.

56. It is the same with the " maroon pure medium " eye. The second line being reserved for the indication of the reflection of the periphery, *without reference to the pigmentation*, and the eyes of this kind being entirely covered by maroon, the periphery line (2) is therefore left blank. Indicate this absence of notation in a similar manner as for the impigmented eye. Thus:

Maroon medium,   or mar. m.
   "   "   "   "
Limited greenish.   lim. gr.

Again:

Maroon pure medium, or mar. pure m.
 "   "   "   "   "   "
    Frank   fr.

CHAPTER II.

COLOR OF THE HAIR AND BEARD.

1. The different shades of color of the hair and beard are more easily ranged and classified than the colors of the eye.

Between the two extremes of the color scale, the *very light blonde* on one hand and the *pure* or *raven black* on the other, are found all the shades of *chestnut* hair.

The complete scale presents itself in about the following order:

BLONDE { *Light and sometimes Flaxen,* *Medium,* *Deep or dark.*

CHESTNUT { *Light,* *Medium,* *Dark.*

CHESTNUT BLACK.

PURE OR RAVEN BLACK.

2. Red hair and beards, which find no place in the above scale, are classed by themselves, and are described according to their shade, as follows:

BRICK RED, SANDY RED, (*blonde red,*) AUBURN, (*chestnut red,*) } *Light, medium and dark.*

3. It is important to distinguish *pure or raven black* from *chestnut black*—commonly called "black" or "dark brown."

"Pure black" hair is rather scarce among white people, except perhaps with Spaniards or races descendent from them.

4. *Dark chestuut* and *chestnut black* are distinct shades, although near enough alike to occasion confusion, particularly

when observed under artificial light. These are the shades of a fresh common chestnut.

5. *Chestnut medium* and *chestnut light* are each one grade lighter than the preceding.

6. The distinction between *light chestnut* and *deep blonde* is a delicate one. One is unconsciously led, sometimes, to describe as dark blonde on a woman what he would designate as light chestnut on a man.

7. *Medium blonde* and *light blonde* need not be defined.

8. The expressions, *very light blonde* and *flaxen*, might sometimes be used to advantage to designate the exceptionally light color of hair of people from the north of Europe (Scandinavians).

9. We may remark that we have purposely avoided the use of the word "brown," which is always a vague expression. Hair called "brown" corresponds generally to what we call *dark chestnut* or *chestnut black*. The same word (brown) applied to the color of the beard is frequently used to designate a mixture of black with red chestnut hairs.

In painting, the word "brown" is applied to the color of a dark chestnut shading on black, and generally to any color much darkened by black.

10. *Gray* hair, which cannot properly have an assigned place in the color scale, may be divided into two classes:

$$\text{GRAY} \begin{cases} Dark, \\ Medium, \\ Light. \end{cases} according\ as\ it\ approaches\ white$$

GRAY MIXED.

In the first mentioned class may be placed all heads of hair that have turned gray to such an extent that their original color has disappeared, or become undistinguishable.

The term *gray mixed* may be applied to hair the proper color of which is still discernible but which is largely interspersed with gray. When the natural color predominates the expression "gray mixed," should be added to the name of the shade.

In the like manner *turning gray, gray on temples, etc.*, may be employed advantageously as occasion may arise.

CHAPTER III.

NOTATION OF THE PROFILE AND DIMENSIONS OF THE NOSE.

1. The nose is the feature to which every human face owes its distinguishing peculiarity.

Its varieties of form (A) and dimensions (B) present an infinite number of combinations, which current language has reduced to four or five leading types, easily recognizable when their characteristics are well defined.

Unfortunately the intermediate forms, more often met with than the typical forms, do not enter readily into these divisions. Descriptive epithets will enable us, however, to give a strict definition of all imaginable cases.

A—Form of the Nose.

3. Let us first say a word or two about the parts that compose the nose:

4. *The root of the nose* (X) is that transverse depression, more or less marked, found at the top of the nose, between the eyes and just below the base of the forehead—(Fig 22, G.) The *sub-nasal point* is the inner angle, situated on the median line, formed by the junction of the *base of the nose* and upper lip. The upper part of the nose is hard and bony; it has a skeleton of its own formed by the *nasal bones.* The *wings* of the nose are the two side parts of the *lobule* which limit the openings of the *nostrils,* and which are separated from the cheek by a *furrow,* more or less *rounded,* more or less *deep,* more or less *compressed.*

5. The point or *tip* of the nose is the most prominent point of the lobule. The *ridge* of the nose is the profile line of the

nose from its root to its tip. The lower extremity or *base* of the nose extends from the tip to the sub-nasal point.

6. In the *profile* of the nose are distinguished:

    I. The general form of the *ridge* of the nose.

    II. The inclination of its *base*.

    III. The particular form of the *root*.

I. The general form of the ridge of the nose is expressed by the five following terms:

First. CONCAVE.—The upper part, which corresponds to the bone of the nose, descends more or less obliquely in an almost straight line; then the lower part, corresponding to the lobule, curves outward in such a manner that the whole ridge of the nose presents in profile a concave form. (Fig. 22, A. F. K.)

Second. RECTILINEAL.—The ridge of the nose describes an almost *straight* line from root to tip. (Fig. 22, B. G. L.)

Third. CONVEX.—The ridge of the nose describes a convex curve almost uniform from root to tip. (Fig. 22, C. H. M.)

Fourth. HUMPED.—The upper part of the bony portion presents a short and decided convexity, below which the remainder of the bony portion becomes almost straight, the inclination being continued without interruption or inflexion along the back of the lobule. (Fig. 22, D. I. N.) The humped nose may be regarded as a variety of the convex.

Fifth. UNDULATED.—The upper part is convex, but the profile of the lobule, instead of continuing this curve as in the "aquiline" or "Roman" nose, or of taking a rectilineal direction as in the "humped," bends inward. The result is that the direction of the line is convex above, and concave below the bony portion, becoming necessarily convex again toward the tip. It is therefore undulated (Fig. 22, E. J. O.) The *undulated* should be considered as a variety of the *concave, rectilineal* or *humped* noses according as its ridge may present in general a hollowed, straight or humped outline. *Therefore the qualificative* UNDULATED *should always be followed by the words* CONCAVE, HUMPED *or* RECTILINEAL *as the case may be.*

    EXAMPLE —Undulated Rectilineal, Undulated Concave Undulated Humped.

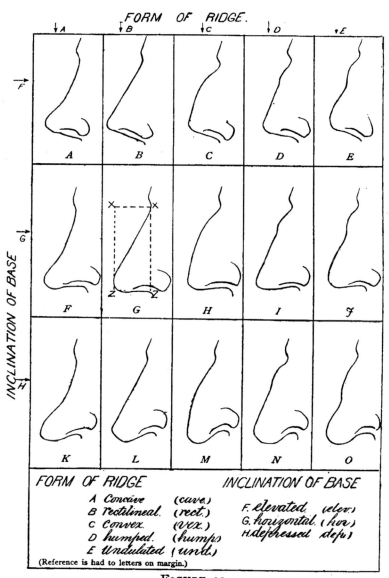

FIGURE 22.
THE NOSE.
FORM AND INCLINATION.

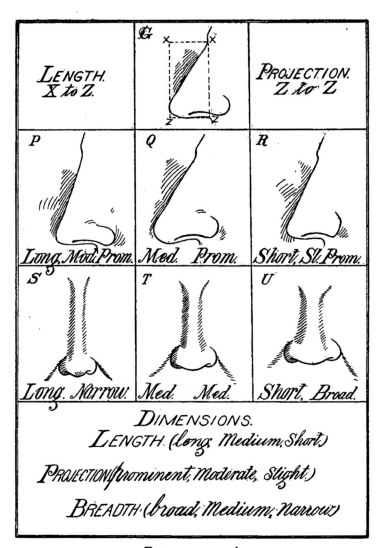

FIGURE 22.—2d.

THE NOSE.

DIMENSIONS.

When a nose is but slightly undulated and at same time very concave, or decidedly humped, it would naturally be classified as "humped" or "concave," the expression *slightly undulated* being added.

II. The *inclination* of the base of the nose may be *Elevated* (Fig. 22, A. to E.), *Horizontal* (Fig. 22, F. to J.), or *Depressed* (Fig. 22, K. to O.) These words are self-explanatory.

III. The particular form of the cavity at the *root* of the nose may be described as *shallow* or *deep*, with base *wide* or *narrow*.

7. The words denoting the inclination of the base—*Elevated, horizontal* or *depressed*—should be coupled, according to the case, with one of the five terms assigned to the ridge. *Concave, rectilineal, convex, humped, undulated.*

8. EXAMPLE.—Nose concave with the base elevated (Fig. 22, A.) or, for greater rapidity, concave nose elevated; or, again, humped depressed (Fig. 22, N.) Rectilineal horizontal (Fig. 22, G.), etc.

9. Although the employment of the two epithets is indispensable, it must not be supposed that in practice all the terms of one division can be combined with all in the other divisions and in the same proportion.

10. Certain combinations are much more frequently met with than others.

11. The undulated nose, for instance, is very often depressed (Francis I type), (Fig. 22, O.)

12. The concave nose has ordinarily an elevated base, (familiarly called a "turned up" nose), (Fig. 22, A.); while the base of the convex nose is either horizontal (Jewish type, Fig. 22, H.), or depressed ("hooked," like a parrot's beak), (Fig. 22, M.), etc.

13. The rectilineal nose with horizontal base, and with a root but slightly defined, constitutes the classic nose of the Greek statuary.

14. A convex nose with base elevated is exceptional, and a concave nose with base depressed, still more so. (Fig. 22, K.)

15. The combinations instanced in the foregoing para-

graphs are of the two divisions, *ridge* and *base.* With the exception of *undulated ridges* (paragraph 6, No. 5) there will seldom be occasion for coupling two qualificatives of the same division.

16. For forms in transition from one type of nose to another, it is advisable to have recourse to the method of sublineation and parentheses similarly used in designating the color of the eyes.

17. Thus a nose *convex depressed* (convex underlined), implies a nose exceedingly convex (Fig. 22, M.); while (convex) *depressed*—(convex in parenthesis) signifies slightly convexed, almost a straight nose. Same difference between *undulated* and (undulated.)

18. The underline will represent always the emphatic form, and the parenthesis, the form less pronounced—*approaching* the *rectilineal* for the ridge of the nose, and the *horizontal* for the base.

19. The parentheses permit you to restrict the use of the words rectilineal and horizontal to ridges positively straight and bases exactly horizontal.

B.—*Dimensions.* (Fig. 22, 2d.)

20. Having spoken of *form*, it now remains for us to treat of that other element of every solid—*dimensions.*

21. For the sake of clearness in the notation, it is important to have these two points of view distinctly separated.

22. The three dimensions of the nose are its *length, projection*, and *breadth.*

23. The meaning of these expressions should be determined.

24. The length is not measured along the ridge of the nose as might naturally be supposed. It is the perpendicular line X Z (Fig. 22, 2d G.), from the root of the nose to the sub-nasal point. The illusion of apparently increased length in noses with depressed bases, which always seem longer than they really are, and of decreased length in elevated noses which always seem short, is thus avoided.

25. The *projection* of the nose is the distance from the most salient point of the tip to the perpendicular line X. Z. (G.)

26. The *breadth* is the greatest transverse distance between the two wings.

27. The direct measurement of the three dimensions by means of compasses would present certain difficulties in execution. The operator may therefore content himself with noting on a second line, under the heading *Peculiarities*, dimensions that are very far removed either way from the average.

28. The abbreviation "m" (for medium) under *dimensions* will explain the absence of any observation of this kind.

29. Considered with reference to its three dimensions, a nose may be *long, medium* or *short* (Fig. 22, 2d P. Q. R.); with a projection *prominent, moderately prominent*, or *slightly prominent* (Fig. 22, 2d P. Q. R.); and lastly, with respect to its breadth, *broad, medium* or *narrow* (Fig. 22, 2d S. T. U.)

The term *flat* is applied only to noses that are broad and but slightly prominent. The word *crushed* may be used for noses flattened by an accident.

30. *Large, slender* and *pointed* are applied especially to the point of the lobule—(tip of the nose)—the peculiarity being noted only when very marked.

31. *The words* LARGE *and* SMALL, *as embracing all of the three dimensions, should never be employed.*

32. By employing the above adjectives in the order observed, and exclusively for the special designations assigned to them, you avoid a repetition in each indication of the words: Length, breadth and height. If it is understood, for instance, that the adjective *large* shall be employed only for the tip of the nose, a *nose large* would necessarily signify a nose with a large or fleshy tip.

33. Under the heading *Peculiarities* should appear any malformation or peculiarity worthy of note that cannot properly be placed under the divisions *Profile* and *Dimensions*.

34. We instance: "Nose twisted to the right (or left)," pimpled nose, red nose, root of the nose very pronounced (or scarcely defined) tip of the nose large (or pointed), etc.

35. The seven observations following are especially to be noted.

1st. The slight swelling in the form of an elongated olive, situated at the junction of the nasal bone with the cartilage and about two centimeters below the root, forming what is known as the *bridge* of the nose. The swelling does not show as a protuberance on the ridge when seen in profile, but when viewed full face, and if very pronounced, it gives the nose a special character. It may be noted in the " peculiarities " as *bridge flat* (or *wide.*)

2d. A flat, triangular place noticed sometimes on the end of the nose—the two nasal cartilages on reaching the tip seem to bifurcate—which may be described by the words: *End of nose flat;* or again, when each cartilage makes a distinct ridge or protuberance under the skin : *End of nose bi-lobed.*

3d. A nose with *sub-partition* exposed. The partition of the nose is the cartilage that separates the nostrils from each other. Its lower edge is generally seen. A nose is said to have its *partition exposed* when the cartilage extends considerably below the lower limit of each nostril.

This peculiarity is frequently met with in convex noses of the Jewish type. It should be noted only when very pronounced.

4th. The nose generally known as the " classic Greek " (described also, but wrongfully, as a straight nose) draws its characteristic from the combination of a *rectilineal horizontal* profile (with three medium dimensions), having the root but slightly marked—(shallow)—with a forehead having the same inclination as the ridge of the nose.

5th. We have now to speak of the relation of the nose to the regions adjoining.

Does the lower portion of the face project? If the jaws, (or the upper jaw only) extend forward, the lower part of the nose will be thrown in the same direction; and the more marked the projection the greater will be the angle formed by the line of the ridge with the vertical.

This peculiarity should also be noted by some appropriate

formula : *Projection of the jaws, projection of the upper jaw, of the middle of the upper jaw;* or again, under the general formula of *prominence of the lower part of the face*—there being no need of mentioning the exaggerated inclination of the ridge of the nose resulting therefrom.

6th. It is the same with the angle formed by the ridge of the nose and profile of the forehead.

The *forehead*, considered with regard to its inclination, may be either *convex* or *straight* (or perpendicular), *slightly receding or very receding.*

The angle made by the nose and forehead will, of course, increase proportionately, and there will be no necessity to note it.

7th. The *nostrils* also give cause for some special observations. They may be *pinched* or *wide*. Their openings become *oval* in the first case, and more or less *round* in the second. When this latter form is plainly apparent it is a noteworthy characteristic.

We cannot repeat too often that the various peculiarities enumerated in the preceding paragraphs should be noted only when very pronouned.

A notation of the profile and dimensions conformably with the vocabulary of appellations is quite sufficient for the requirements of a good description in the majority of cases, without any additional notes.

APPROXIMATION AND LIMITATION OF POSSIBLE DEVIATIONS.

37. The series of qualificatives describing the direction of the ridge of the nose is presented in the following order:

<u>Concave</u>, Concave, (Concave.)

Rectilineal, } (*Humped*), *humped*, <u>humped.</u>
        (*Convex*), *convex,* <u>convex.</u>

Each term in this progression could be confounded, according to the case, with the term preceding or following, without the observer being at fault. It would be considered an error, however, if he should step over one class and into the next. Thus (*concave*), signifying *slightly concave*, might be confounded with *rectilineal*, but not with *slightly humped—(humped)* —nor *slightly convex—(convex.)*

In like manner the confusing of *concave*—(underlined) with *(concave)*—(in parenthesis) would constitute a fault.

In Undulated Ridges a super-position of the serial order might occur. Thus a nose *undulated (concave)* might be characterized at a subsequent observation as *undulated rectilineal*, but not as *undulated humped*. In the same way each term of the class *slightly undulated—(undulated)* might be confounded with the corresponding group of *non-undulated*.

38. The series of the Inclination of the Base which presents neither bifurcation nor super-position is more simple still.

It commences with the form the most elevated and descends progressively to the most depressed:

Elevated, elevated (elevated), horizontal, (depressed) depressed, depressed.

Thanks to the intermediate terms, it is difficult to confound *exceedingly elevated* with *slightly elevated*, or this latter with *slightly depressed*.

39. It is the same with the qualificatives of *dimension*. The series *long, medium, short*, and *prominent, moderately prominent, slightly prominent*, as well as *broad, medium, narrow*, may also present a like super-position or confusion of contiguous terms. In this division the seven term series with parentheses and underlines may be omitted. Its use, however, is optional with the observer.

In any case, the confusion or transposition of two extreme qualificatives is not possible: what is narrow, for instance, for one observer, may be regarded as medium by another, but not as broad.

So, no matter what the class under consideration may be, the discrepancies (we will not say errors) between two observers will be confined within very narrow limits, which can, *a priori*, be defined exactly for each case taken separately.

In order to be proficient, it is necessary to have at the tongue's command the serial order, either ascending or descending, of the various terms in the several divisions.

ABBREVIATIONS.

40. The employment of the following abbreviations permits greater rapidity in writing. The narrowness of the columns of the descriptive card, moreover, renders the use of them almost indispensable. It is hardly necessary to say, however, that all descriptive extracts furnished at the command of the courts, or at the request of other prison authorities, should have the words written out in full.

Rectilineal, rect.
Concave, cave.   Horizontal, hor.
Convex, vex.   Elevated, elev.
Humped, hump.   Depressed, dep.
Undulated, und.

Prominent, prom.
Slightly   "   sl. p.

Long, short, broad, narrow, large, flat, slender, need not be abbreviated.

SPECIMENS OF A FEW NOSE FORMULAS.

Rect. hor.   Rect. elev.
m. m. m.   m. prom. broad.

Rect. hor.   (Und. hump.) dep.
Short m. broad.   m. m. m.

Cave. hor.   Und. cave. elev.
m. m. m.   Short. flat. broad.

Vex. hor.   Vex. hump. dep.
m. prom. m.   Long m. m.

(Cave) elev.
Long. sl. p. m.

PART THIRD.

Every individual mark should be described with respect to :
1. Its nature (or designation.)
2. Its direction (or inclination.)
3. Its dimensions.
4. Its situation with regard to one or two specified points of the body.

CHAPTER I.

DESIGNATION, INCLINATION, AND DIMENSIONS OF THE MARK TO BE DESCRIBED.

I. NATURE OR DESIGNATION.

1. A scar may be caused by a finger cut, an abscess or a carbuncle, or again, by a knife-thrust, gun-shot wound, burn, etc.

2. When the prisoner's account of the origin of the scar seems probable it should be noted on the descriptive list; but the word " scar " may, for the sake of rapidity, be omitted.

---

*NOTE.—We make no special mention of *tattoo-marks*, which are generally described with sufficient accuracy by the prison receiving officer. They ought, however, to be given an equal place with the others in the descriptive notes, although their value for the purpose of identification is always less than that of scars, moles, etc.

A tattoo mark may always be worked over, and to a certain extent obliterated ; a scar is unchangeable.

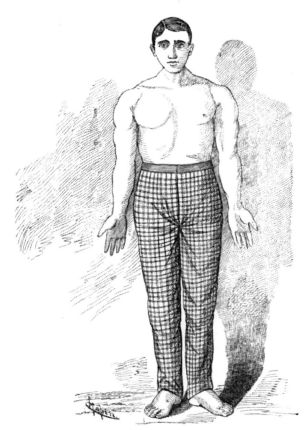

FIGURE 23.

FRONT FACE.

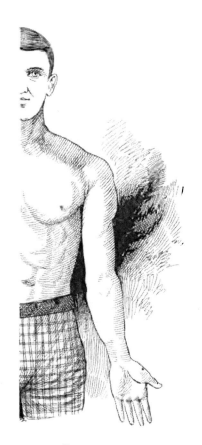

FIGURE 24.

LEFT HALF OF THE FRONT FACE
OF THE BODY.

For instance; "Abscess under middle of right jaw," instead of "scar from abscess," etc. "Carbuncle on breast," etc., instead of "scar from carbuncle," etc.

3. The customary names given to birthmarks will convey a sufficiently clear idea of their appearance without further description. We mention: "Strawberry mark," "coffee," "fly," "cock's crest," etc.

4. The *consideration which ought to take precedence* of all others in picking out the scars and marks to be noted, is that of their *duration* or *permanency*.

The worst mistake an observer can make is to note down as indelible an identifying mark which may disappear or be effaced.

5. When in doubt regarding the permanency of a mark, the word *transient* should be added, followed by a query (?), or in case of a scar not yet closed, the word "*fresh.*"

II. DIRECTION OR INCLINATION.

6. A mark, and particularly a scar, may have a *vertical, oblique,* or *horizontal* inclination, and a *rectilineal, curved, oval, circular, undulated* or *oblong* form, or may present the appearance of *broken lines,* or a cross, or of the letters *V. Z. X.,* etc.*

7. To determine the direction of scars situated on the arms and hands, stand the subject to be examined in the position of a "soldier without arms:" the body erect, the arms hanging naturally at the sides. (Fig. 23.)

8. It is unnecessary to say that scar points, round scars, moles, etc., have no direction.

9. In the description of scars, a relative exactness must not be assigned to the words *horizontal, oblique* and *vertical.* In a strict sense no scar is as horizontal as a water-level or as vertical as a plumb-line. If such a precise signification were attached to the words, all scars would then be styled oblique, and that word would lose its entire value.

NOTE.—A sketch of the scar may be drawn, if deemed necessary.

10. In doubtful cases the difficulty may be overcome by describing the scars as *horizontal-oblique* or *oblique-vertical*, etc.

11. When describing rectilineal-oblique scars, distinguish between *obliquely inward* and *obliquely outward* or *obliquely forward* and *obliquely backward*, according to the direction the scar would take, inward or outward, forward or backward, if lengthened in imagination from the highest point downward, supposing the subject to be standing in the position of a "soldier without arms," (see Section 1 of Chapter II.) For *curved* scars, note which way the concave side, or *cavity* faces. A curved line, the general direction of which is horizontal, may have either an *upward cavity* or *downward cavity;* if it is vertical, these terms become *front* or *rear*, *inner* or *outer*, as the case may be.

If it is oblique, the cavity is to be regarded as neither upward nor downward.

III. DIMENSIONS.

12. The unit of measure for scars is the centimeter; thus, one, two, three centimeters will be written; 1, 2, 3, etc.; and one, two, three millimeters: 0.1—0.2—0.3.

13. Length and breadth are indicated either in centimeters or millimeters as the case may be, an absolute exactness not being essential.

14. In these descriptions the centimeters and millimeters are rarely coupled. A scar may be 4, 5 or 6 millimeters, or 1, 2 or 3 centimeters; but a scar measuring exactly 5 centimeters 7 millimeters would be noted as having a length of 6 centimeters.

15. When the scar is round, the diameter only is indicated; but when oblique or oval the two diameters must be given.

16. Scars and cuts on the fingers should be carefully noted as soon as it becomes evident that the forms they have assumed will be lasting.

17. When their number exceeds three or four for both hands, the principal ones only need be noted. Furthermore,

for this class of scars no dimensions are indicated except those that exceed, either in length or breadth, the ordinary limits. The scarcely visible marks that may be passed by for a subsequent examination may be noted as *slight*.

18. The same may be said of moles, beauty spots, etc. They are so numerous on some individuals that a description of each one of them would be impossible. In such cases the principal ones only are described; the words, "and many others," being added. When expedient, their diameter, general appearance, etc., may be noted. For instance: "Hairy mole on————."

CHAPTER II.

SITUATION OF THE MARKS TO BE DESCRIBED.

SECTION I.

WHAT IS MEANT BY FRONT AND REAR, INNER AND OUTER FACES.

19.   Whatever part of the human body we may consider, it will be recognized as having *four faces: Front, rear* and two *sides.*

20.   Taking the trunk for example, the front face will be represented by the breast, the rear face by the back, and the side faces by the right and left sides. (Figs. 23 and 24.)

21.   For the members, the side faces may be distinguished as *inner* and *outer,* according as they may be turned toward or away from the individual. (Fig, 25.)

22.   In making this distinction for the upper members it is taken for granted, as was suggested in the Chapter on Inclination, that the examined subject is placed in the position of a "soldier without weapons;" his arms hanging full length at the sides, his little fingers pressed against the seams of his trousers, and the palms of his hands *turned completely to the front,* that is to say, on a plane parallel with his face and breast.

23.   In this position the inner angle of the elbow, the palm of the hand and the fleshy side of the fingers are regarded as having a *front face,* while the elbow, the back of the hand and backs of the fingers, nails included, are considered as having a *rear face.*

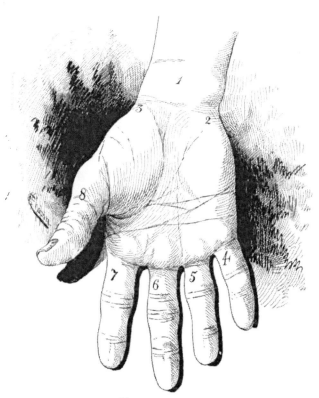

FIGURE 25.

1. Front Face of the Right Hand.
2. Inner Face.
3. Outer Face.
4. Little Finger.
5. Third or Ring Finger.
6. Middle Finger.
7. Index or Fore Finger.
8. Thumb.

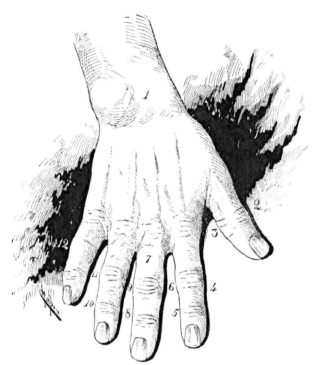

FIGURE 26.

1. Rear Face of the Right Hand.
2. Outer Face of the Right Thumb.
3. Inner Face of the Right Thumb.
4. Outer Face of the Right Fore Finger.
5. Inner Face of the Right Fore Finger.
6. Outer Face of the Right Middle Finger.
7. Rear Face of the Right Middle Finger.
8. Inner Face of the Right Middle Finger.
9. Outer Face of the Right Third Finger.
10. Inner Face of the Right Third Finger.
11. Outer Face of the Right Little Finger.
12. Inner Face of the Right Little Finger.

24. The *inner face* extends from the arm-pit to the little finger, and the *outer face* from the shoulder to the thumb.

25. The faces of each finger are designated on the same principle, according as they may be turned toward or away from the individual.

26. Taking the middle finger for example, the face which, in the position of a "soldier without arms" already described, is turned to the front, is called the *front face of the middle finger*, the reverse the *rear face*; while the face that touches the fore-finger, is styled the *outer face*, and that which touches the third finger the *inner face*. Inversely, the side of the third finger touching the middle finger is termed the *outer face of the third finger*, and the corresponding side of the fore-finger, the *inner side of the fore-finger*. (Fig. 26.)

27. It should be observed that in consequence of the use of the words outer and inner the terms of description will be identically the same, whether the right or left hand be examined. These expressions have the further advantage of doing away with the repetition and juxtaposition of the words right and left in such formulas as "the left face of the right middle finger," "the right face of the right third finger," etc. By analogy, and in order to avoid the disagreeable and confusing repetition of the words right and left, the terms *in front of* and *behind* are often used in their place.

For instance: "Mole, 8 centimeters behind (or in front of) right nipple," or "in front of and above the seventh vertebræ."

28. In practice, for the sake of rapidity, the word "face" is suppressed.

EXAMPLE.—"Left fore-finger outer," instead of "left fore-finger outer face."

SECTION II.

SPECIAL DESIGNATION OF THE DIFFERENT PARTS OF THE BODY
—TERMS AND ANOMALIES PECULIAR TO EACH.

29. In describing peculiar marks, the following order of situation should be observed:

I. Left arm and fore-arm and then left hand.
II. Right arm and fore-arm and then right hand.
III. Face, ears and front of the neck.
IV. Breast and fore-part of the shoulders.
V. Back of the neck and region of the back.
VI. Other parts of the body exhibiting irregularities worthy of note.

30. By making it a rule always to begin with an upper left member before passing to the right, and in general with the left half of the body before the right, you diminish the chances of confusion, always prejudicial, arising from the use of the words right and left.

Each of the six divisions enumerated in the foregoing paragraph should appear in its proper place in the description of scars, *with its Roman numeral in the margin*, and should be separated from the divisions preceding and following, by a horizontal line.

I—II. ARMS, FORE-ARMS AND HANDS (RIGHT AND LEFT).

31. *a.* The *arm* begins at the shoulder and ends at the elbow. The *elbow*, considered with regard to its four faces, may be analyzed as follows: Elbow proper or *elbow rear* (face), *elbow inner* (face), *elbow outer* (face), and *inside angle of the elbow*, which, by analogy and for the sake of abbreviation, we call *elbow front* (face). (Fig. 27.)

32. There are two extremities, shoulder and elbow, that serve as measuring or locating points in describing the situation of a scar on the arm.

EXAMPLES.—Horizontal rectilineal scar of 4 centimeters, 10 centimeters above left elbow front—(Fig. 27). Mole, 5 centimeters below left shoulder outer.

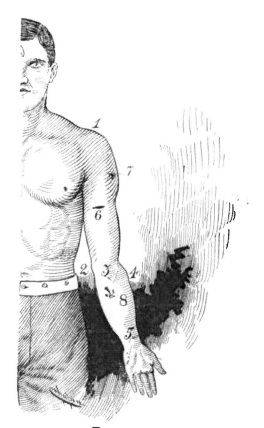

FIGURE 27.

LEFT HALF OF THE FRONT FACE OF THE BODY.

1. Left shoulder.
2. Left elbow. Inner (face).
3. Left elbow. Front (").
4. Left elbow. Outer (").
5. Left fore-arm. Front (").

6. Horizontal Rectilineal Scar, 4 cm.—
   10 cm. above left elbow front.
7. Mole 5 cm. below left shoulder, outer.
8. Tattooed anchor, 3 x 2 cm.—14 cm.
   above left wrist front.

FIGURE 28.

1. Palm.	6.	Little Finger.
2. Thumb.	7.	First Joint.
3. Fore Finger.	8.	Second Joint.
4. Middle Finger.	9.	Third Joint.
5. Third Finger.		

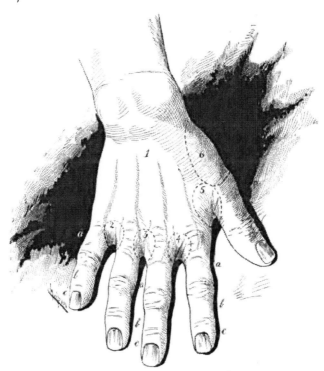

FIGURE 29.

Rear face of the Right Hand.

1. Back of the Hand.
2. Between third and little Fingers.
3. "   middle and third "
4. "   fore and middle "
5. "   thumb and fore "

6. Base of Thumb.
A. First Phalanx of Fingers.
B. Second "   "
C. Third "   "

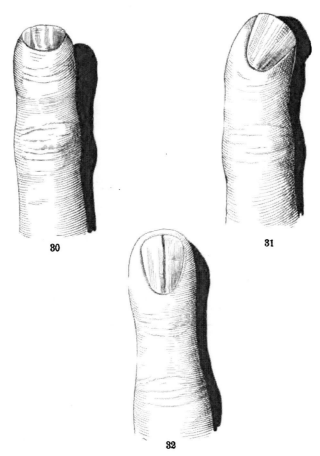

FIGURES 30, 31, 32.

ANOMALIES OF THE FINGERS

30. Shortened Finger.
31. Nail deviated and thickened.
32. Striated or split nail.

33. *b.* The *fore-arm* extends from the elbow to the wrist—two locating points that serve in the same capacity for the fore-arm as the shoulder and elbow do for the arm proper.

EXAMPLES.—Anchor tattooed, 3 centimeters by 2, 14 centimeters above left wrist front—(Fig. 27.)

34. *c.* The upper part of the *hand* may be divided into:
    1st. The *front face*—the palm.
    2d. The *rear face*—the back of the hand, fingers not included.

Then come the fingers, viz.: *Thumb, fore-finger, middle finger, third* or *ring-finger* and *little finger* (Fig. 28).

35. Each finger, thumb excepted, is composed of three *phalanges*, united to one another by *joints.*

36. ☞ *Conformably to scientific usage, but contrary to popular custom, we will in enumerating the phalanges commence at the upper extremities of the fingers: 1st phalanx and 1st joint, 2d phalanx and 2d joint, 3d phalanx and 3d joint. The first joint* is therefore contiguous in *front* to the *palm,* and in *rear* to the *back of the hand.*

37. The *thumb* has but two phalanges and two joints. The part of the hand that unites it to the wrist, has, for greater rapidity in practice, received the name of *base of the thumb* or *thumb-base.*

38. The intervals between the fingers are known as: *Between thumb and first, between first and second, between second and third, between third and little fingers.* (Fig. 29.)

Between thumb and fore-finger rear is very often the seat of small tattoo marks (anchors, hearts, initials, etc.,) which should not be overlooked.

39. The fingers may have one, two, or three phalanges amputated.

40. Often the last phalanx has simply a piece cut off, without being actually amputated; in such a case the finger is said to be *shortened.* (Fig. 30.)

41. Cases where the stump of a nail is more or less twisted, or has deviated, should also be carefully noted. (Fig. 31.)

Fingers that have previously been crushed have sometimes a *thickened nail*. A wound at the root of the nail occasions what we call a *striated or split nail*—a characteristic of frequent oc. currence and of great permanence, and which is easily described,—noted briefly thus: Right middle finger-nail striated. (Fig. 32.)

42. Finally, the finger joints, and in general all the joints, may be *stiffened* or *anchylosed*, either *slightly* or *completely*. In the first-named condition they can be moved but imperfectly; in the latter, not at all. In complete anchylosis it is necessary to state whether the two members are consolidated in a straight line, or at a right or obtuse angle. (See the remarks relative to the measurement of fingers 1st Part, Chap. II.)

III. FACE, EARS AND FRONT OF THE NECK.

43. *a.* It is sufficient to name again, without defining them, the different parts of the face which may be the seat of particular marks, or which may serve as points to indicate their position (Figs. 33, 34.)

44. They are, commencing at the top, the *scalp* and the *line of growth of the hair;* the *frontal bumps (right and left)* and the *cavity at the root of the nose;* then the *eye-brows*, which are divided into :

Inner point of the right or left eye-brow.
Outer point of the right or left eye-brow.
Middle of the right or left eye-brow.

Then follow the *right* and *left* eyes with their *upper* and *lower eyelids* having an *inner* and *outer angle;* the *ridge* and *base of the nose*, which, taken together, form what is called the *profile of the nose.*

The wings of the nose—right and left;
The end or tip of the nose;

The *under part of the nose* and *the nostrils*, the dividing line of which outlines the base of the nose (already named.)

The chin;
The point of the chin;
The under part of the chin.

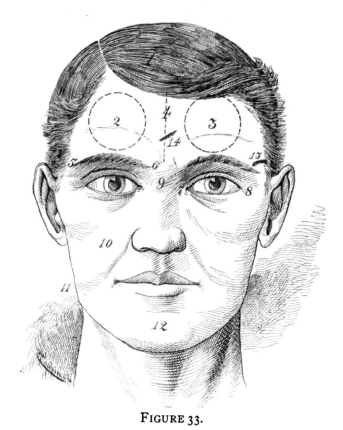

FIGURE 33.

1.	Scalp.	10.	Cheek.
2.	Right frontal bump.	11.	Right jaw.
3.	Left " "	12.	Chin.
4.	Median line, forehead	13.	Scar obliquely forward, downward cavity, 3 centimetres, left temple above outer point eyebrow.
5.	Outer point right eyebrow.		
6.	Inner " " "		
7.	Inner angle of left eye.	14.	Rectilineal scar, right-oblique, 2 cemtimetres, middle of forehead; 4 centimetres above root of nose.
8.	Outer " " "		
9.	Cavity at root of the nose.		

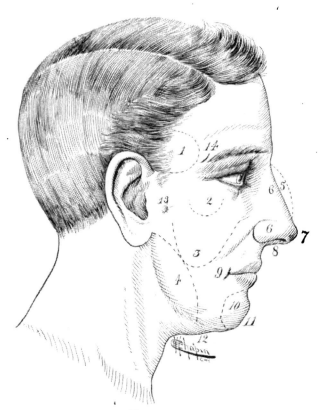

FIGURE 34.

1.	Right Temple.	7.	Point or Tip of the Nose.
2.	Right Cheek Bone.	8.	Base of the Nose.
3.	Right Cheek.	9.	Right Corner of the Mouth.
4.	Right Jaw.	10.	Chin.
5.	Ridge of the Nose.	11.	Point of the Chin.
6.	Right Wing of the Nose.	12.	Under part of the Chin.

13 Mole, 3c. in front of Right Tragus.

14. Scar, right oblique, rectilineal, upward cavity,
1½c., right eye-brow outer.

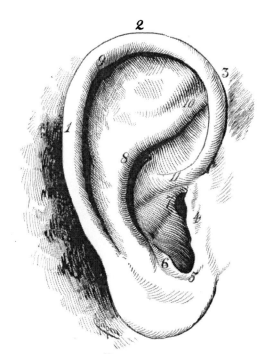

FIGURE 35.

THE EAR.

1.	Lower rim.	7.	Cavity of the shell.
2.	Upper rim.	8.	Rim of the shell.
3.	Front rim.	9.	Furrow of the rim.
4.	Tragus.	10.	Navicular cavity.
5.	Lobe.	11.	Starting point of rim.
6.	Antitragus.		

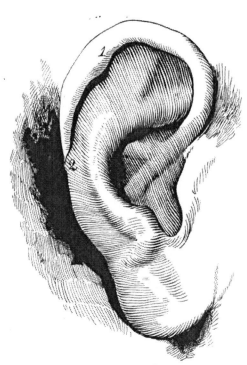

FIGURE 36.

1 Indented.
2. Flattened or bruised.

45. If from the chin we ascend obliquely in the direction of the ear, we will encounter the *base of the cheek* and more particularly, the parts of the maxillary bone known as the *right and left jaw.*

46. Abscesses worthy of note will very often be observed on the necks of scrofulous individuals, situated under the jaw and from five to ten centimeters from the ear.

47. Just above, we find the *cheek* proper, then the *cheek-bone* and, to the rear and higher up, the *temples.*

48. *b.* Having reached the *ear*, we notice the small cartilage of the *tragus*, very convenient as a locating point for the scars of the cheek; then, underneath it, the *lobe of the ear* (which may be wanting); then, above, the *rim of the ear*, which is divided into three parts; *front, upper* and *lower.* (Fig. 35.)

49. The *rim* may be *wanting* or *flattened*, or *notched*, or *bruised*, or may present *nodes* and *indentations*, which, reproduced by photography, are valuable aids in establishing identity. They are always important peculiarities and should, when they present themselves, be included in the list of particular marks. (Fig. 36.)

50. Examples of scars observed on the face:

"Scar obliquely forward, cavity downward, 3 centimeters, left temple."—(Fig. 33.)

"Mole, 3 centimeters in front of right tragus."

"Scar obliquely backward, upward cavity, 1½ centimeters, right eye-brow outer."—(Fig. 34.)

"Scar right oblique, rectilineal, 2 centimeters, middle of forehead, 4 centimeters above root of nose." (Fig. 33.)

51. *c.* On the front of the *neck* is situated *Adam's apple*, familiar to every one, and lower down, just at the top of the breast, is found the *fork of the sternum*—by abbreviation the *fork*, simply—both valuable points for describing the location of the moles, birthmarks and scars that are frequently found in this vicinity.

EXAMPLE.—"Mole, 3 centimeters above fork and 2 centimeters to left of Adam's apple."—(Fig. 37.)

82

IV. BREAST.

52. *a.* The *right* and *left nipples* render a like service for the *breast.*

EXAMPLE.—Mole, 5 centimeters above and in front of right nipple, and 8 centimeters below fork.—(Fig. 37.)

53. When the mark to be described is situated beyond the region of the fork, *the median line* is taken as the second locating point.

EXAMPLE.—Slight scar oblique inward, upward cavity, 5 centimeters (long), 8 centimeters below left nipple, and 10 centimeters from the median line.—(Fig. 37.)

54. By *median line* we understand the imaginary line which divides the human body into two equal and symmetrical parts, and which, in front, passes through the middle of the forehead, the profile of the nose, the chin, the fork, the navel and the crotch. (Fig. 37.)

V. BACK OF THE NECK AND REGION OF THE BACK.

55. *a.* On the back, the median line is represented by the *vertebral column*—abbreviated, *column* or *backbone.* (Fig. 38.)

56. *b.* The second and last locating point for the entire region of the back is the *seventh* or *prominent vertebra.*

EXAMPLE.—Carbuncle, 4 centimeters below 7th and 13 centimeters to left of column.—(Fig. 38.)

The seventh vertebra (by abbreviation " 7th," simply) is situated on the vertebral column, a little above the line of the shoulders. It is quite prominent on lean men, even when the neck is in its normal position. When it is invisible, its location must be determined by feeling with the fingers, or by bending the subject's head forward.

57. It is difficult sometimes to distinguish the seventh vertebra from the sixth or fifth, which may be equally prominent. But the errors that may result from any confusion in this respect are too slight to be noticed.

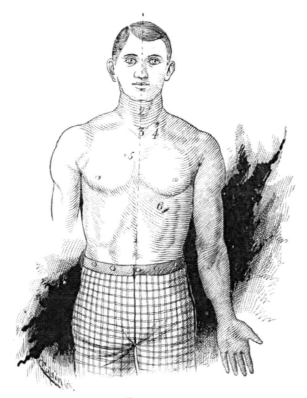

FIGURE 37.

1. Median Line.
2. Adam's Apple.
3. Fork of the Sternum.
4. Mole, 3 cent. above Fork, and 2 cent to left of Adam's Apple.
5. Mole, 12 cent. above right Nipple, and 4 cent. from Median Line.
6. Scar, obliquely inward, slight upward cavity, 5 cent. long, 8 cent. below left Nipple and 10 cent. from Median Line.

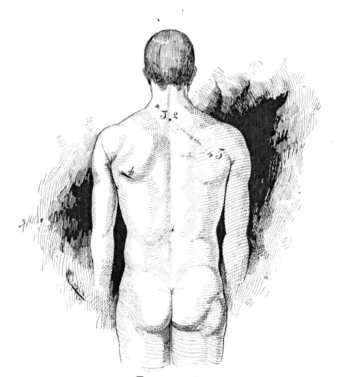

FIGURE 38.

1. Vertebral Column.
2. Seventh Vertebra (7th simply.)
3. Carbuncle, 4 cent. above 7th and 3 cent. to left of Column.
4. Rectilineal Scar, obliquely inward, 4 cent. (long) 30 cent. below 7th, and 13 cent. to left of Column.
5. Mole, 10 cent. to right of Column, 18 cent. below 7th.

VI. ANOMALIES AND INDIVIDUAL MARKS ON OTHER PARTS OF THE BODY.

58. The same method of description, the use of which we have just explained in connection with the upper members and trunk, is equally applicable to the lower members. Its application being much more restricted, however, we will not enter into any details.

59. The observer having familiarized himself with the foregoing examples, will be able to describe easily every case that comes under his notice. He need never hesitate, we may add, to deviate in his descriptions from the rules laid down, and to employ words and expressions in current use whenever those specified in the preceding chapters are not sufficiently precise.

CHAPTER III.

REVIEW AND GENERAL OBSERVATIONS.

60. There is no one who does not bear on his person, in greater or less numbers, and often unknown to himself, some moles or scars. Five or six of these individual marks will suffice to distinguish a man among millions of others, on the *sine qua non* condition, however, that they be minutely described.

61. It is important to remark that one locating point is not sufficient to determine exactly the situation of a particular mark, unless the mark to be noted is found just on the locating point, or very near it.

62. For instance, a mark noted in these terms: *Mole 12 centimeters from right nipple,*—might be situated on any point whatever of the imaginary circumference described around the nipple, with a radius of twelve centimeters. (Fig. 37.)

63. The formula: *Mole, 12 centimeters above right nipple*, is somewhat more exact; the word *above* eliminating more than half of the circumference mentioned.

64. But the situation of the mark is definitely ascertained only by the help of a second locating point; 4 *centimeters from the median line;* or again: 15 *centimeters below the fork of the sternum.*

65. This remark is equally applicable to the region of the back, neck, etc.*

66. We cannot repeat too often that *the importance of particular marks as an indication is directly in proportion to the preciseness of their description.*

The ideal in this respect is attained when a subsequent observer, engaged in similar operations elsewhere, is enabled, by simply reading the description transmitted, to reproduce upon himself tracings imitating exactly, as regards form, situation, dimensions and general appearance, the individual marks described.

The following calculation will impress you with the great interest that results therefrom, regarded from the standpoint of identity.

67. Let us suppose an anthropometric indication containing under the head of *particular marks* these words simply: "*One scar on the breast.*" Certainly this information is not without value. But is it not easy to understand that its descriptive force would have been doubled if this supplementary information had been added: "On the left (or right) half of the breast." As the chances are equal of finding the scar in question on either side of the breast, the indication: "*A scar on the left half of the breast,*" has a descriptive value equivalent to that of "*two scars on the breast*" (without indicating the side.)

68. Let us increase the number of determining words. If, to a "*scar on the left breast*" we add the qualificative *oblique* (or *horizontal* or *vertical*) its value is again doubled, and following the same line of reasoning as in the preceding paragraph,

---

*Note.—For cuts on the hands and limbs, however, and for certain scars on the face, it is generally sufficient to indicate one locating point; especially when it is possible to add the words: Above or below, front or behind, etc.

In this matter some latitude is allowed the observer.

is equivalent to that of an indication worded simply *"four scars on the breast."*

69. In the same way, if we add *"oblique inward"* (there are as many chances that the scar in question may be oblique inward as oblique outward) its descriptive value will be once more doubled, and the notation complete *"scar oblique inward on the left breast"* has the same importance from a descriptive standpoint as the information conveyed in these bare words, *"Eight scars on the breast."*

70. To the determining words mentioned, let us add : *"4 centimeters from the left nipple,"* or better : *"4 centimeters above left nipple,"* or with still greater precision : *"4 centimeters above left nipple, and 10 centimeters from the median line."* (Fig. 37.) To this sentence let us again add the length of the scar, its form and, if ascertained, its origin (knife cut, abscess, burn, etc.,) and we shall have clearly demonstrated, reasoning progressively, that the complete description drawn up in accordance with the rules given in the foregoing pages must, for descriptive or identifying purposes, be equal in value to a formula like the following : *"We note thirty-two (or even sixty-four) scars on the chest of this individual."*

71. *Want of practice alone* prevents us from discerning at a glance the value for identification of a description like this : " Mole on the back, 10 centimeters to the right of the vertebral column, and 18 centimeters below the seventh vertebra." (Fig. 38); while the equivalent formula : " Sixty-four scars on the chest " convinces us at once that but a very limited number of individuals could be found in the entire world similarly scarred.

72. Let five or six peculiarities of this sort, observed on the same individual (they can always be found by close examination) be noted side by side and carefully described, and you will have a collection of proofs of identity that will surpass in certainty all others, whether based on photographs or personal recollections.*

---

*NOTE.—The minimum number of particular marks to be designated on each subject is, we have said, five or six; but it may be expedient occasionally to nearly

73. The following table gives a recapitulation of the indications that a description of individual marks may contain:

Order Numerals	Nature of the Mark.	Form.	Dimensions.	General Inclination.	Situation with respect to one or two locating points.	Face
I. II. III. IV. V. VI.	Scar. Carbuncle. Abscess. Cut. Burn. Birthmark. Mole. Tattoo Marks. Etc.	Rectilineal or Curved. With Cavity. { Upward, Downward or Inward, Outward, Forward, Backward. Triangular, Oval, Round, Half Oval, Crescent, or like letters Z. X. Y. V. etc.	1. 2. 3. 4. for Rectilineal Scars or 3×4, 4×8, etc., for Scars with two dimensions, meaning three centimeters long by four broad, etc.)	Horizontal, Vertical, or Oblique. { Forward, Backward, Inward, Outward. On Curved scars describe which way the Cavity faces.	Above, Below or Under, Middle, On, Across, ——— To right, To left, (of one or two locating points).	Front, Rear, Outer, Inner, (when the mark is situated on one of the members.)

LIST OF ABBREVIATIONS.

In prisons and houses of detention where the daily number of incoming and outgoing prisoners is large, officers charged with the taking of descriptions have found it expedient to

double this limit. When a subject exhibits a great number of scars, it is not possible for you to make identically the same selection that another observer has made or may hereafter make. But agreement in description as regards some of the marks is an indispensable element of identification; hence the necessity of describing nearly all the important ones. Generally the prescribed minimum may easily be completed by examining the lower limbs more carefully than usual. In cases, very rare indeed, where the specified number cannot be reached, the numerical insufficiency should be noted by the formula: "*No others observed.*"

In cases of subjects whose *measurements* are all average ones, have recourse to this formula in the description of scars only after having made a minute and complete examination.

adopt in place of the usual terms a certain number of abbreviations, a list of which is given below. Observers who will familiarize themselves with it will find that its use saves considerable time, which will compensate them for the trouble of learning. We would add, however, that abbreviations of terms other than those enumerated in the list might lead to confusion, and should be avoided.

HAND.	Thumb,	T.
	Forefinger,	F. F.
	Middle Finger,	M. F.
	Third Finger,	T. F.
	Little Finger,	L. F.
	Phalanx,	Ph.
	Joint,	J.
	Wrist,	W.
FACES AND SITUATION.	Inward,	Inw
	Inner,	In.
	Outward,	Outw
	Outer,	Out.
	Forward,	Forw.
	Backward,	Bkw.
	Front,	
	Rear,	
	Downward,	Down.
	Upward,	Up.
	Above.	
	Below.	
	Under,	Und.
	Right,	R.
	Left,	L.
INCLINATION.	Oblique,	Obl.
	Horizontal,	Hor.
	Vertical,	Vert.
SUNDRY.	Scar,	Sc.
	Rectilineal,	Rect.
	Curved,	Curv.
	With Cavity,	Cav.
	Anchylosed,	Anch. (or K.)
	Carbuncle,	Carb.
	Mole,	Mole.
	Forehead,	F'h'd.
	Centimeter,	Ct. (or C.)

APPENDIX.

PHOTOGRAPHS.

INSTRUCTIONS AS TO THE MANNER OF TAKING PHOTOGRAPHS
INTENDED TO BE FILED WITH CARDS OF DESCRIPTION
AND MEASUREMENT IN AN ANTHROPOMETRIC
COLLECTION

1. The prisoner should be photographed *full-face* and *profile*, the following conditions as to reduction, pose, light, and mounting being observed.

I. REDUCTION.

2. In selecting the camera objective and in placing the camera and posing chair in position, the purpose to be accomplished is to have a length of twenty centimeters on the face of the subject to be photographed show upon the negative a reduced image of three centimeters (thirty millimeters).

3. The relative positions of the chair and camera can be quickly found with the help of an assistant, who, seated on the posing chair, will hold perpendicularly against his face a small wooden rule to which a white strip of paper two hundred millimeters long has been fastened.

The photographer will then move his apparatus either way until the twenty-centimeter strip held by the assistant gives on the ground glass of the camera a reduced image of thirty millimeters, which he can verify by a measuring card held in readiness.

4. The ascertained distance should be marked by small cleats fastened to the floor, which will allow the chair and camera to be replaced quickly in their respective positions.

II. POSE.

5. Each subject should be photographed exactly :
  1. *Full-face.*
  2. *Profile* (right side), the head being held in such a

position that the eyes will be horizontal, and looking straight to the front.

6. Be careful for both poses to have the subject squarely and firmly seated, his shoulders of an even height, his head resting against the support.

7. For the profile, seat the subject sideways, closely against the back of the chair, in such a manner that both the head and body will present a perfect side aspect, the left arm, which should hang over the back of the chair, being invisible.

Without this precaution the "profile" would be nearer the camera than the "full-face," and would give a noticeably larger image.

III. LIGHT.

9. The light thrown upon the full-face pose should come from the left of the subject, his right side remaining in comparative shade.

10. For the "profile" a light falling perpendicularly on the head is needed.

IV. GENERAL REMARKS.

11. The register number of the subject should be conspicuously fastened to his coat, to prevent an after confusion or misplacement of the proofs.

12. As the interest in the "profile" is confined chiefly to the indication of the slope of the forehead, the outline of the nose and the shape of the ear, the subject's hair should be cut closely, or be well brushed back.

13. The ear should be entirely exposed, and all profile negatives that do not sharply show its complete outline, ought to be thrown aside, and new ones taken.

V. SIZE AND MOUNTING OF THE PROOFS.

14. The proofs should be cut and mounted in the place assigned them on the card of measurements, the "profile" on the left side, the "full-face" on the right. As much of the bust should be shown as the negative will admit of.

15. *The negatives should never, for any reason whatsoever, be retouched or altered.*

CPSIA information can be obtained at www.ICGtesting.com
Printed in the USA
BVOW05s1413081015

421623BV00013B/34/P